D1348530

IMPROVE YOUR
SNOOKER

IMPROVE YOUR SNOOKER

Willow Books
Collins
8 Grafton Street, London W1
1987

Willow Books
William Collins Sons & Co Ltd
London · Glasgow · Sydney · Auckland
Toronto · Johannesburg

First published 1987
©Sackville Design Group Ltd

BRITISH LIBRARY CATALOGUING IN PUBLICATION DATA
Improve your Snooker
1. Snooker
I. Everton, Clive
794.7′35   GV900.S6

ISBN 0-00-218255-6

Designed by Sackville Design Group Ltd
78 Margaret Street, London W1N 7HB
Introduction and break analyses: Clive Everton
Text: Edward Horton
Art director: Al Rockall
In-house editor: Lorraine Jerram
Illustrations: Phil Evans
Designers: Phil Evans
Stephen Rogala-Kaluski
Set in Melior by Thomas/Weintroub Associates, Wembley
Printed and bound in Italy by New Interlitho S.P.A. Milan

Contents

Play better snooker

Snooker is the great sporting success story of modern times, but it is easily forgotten that it was a very substantial folk sport long before it became a normal subject for dinner-table conversation. There were three million players in Britain alone even when the World Professional Championship had sunk so low in public interest that it was not held at all from 1950 to 1964, and for five years thereafter only on a limited challenge basis.

By 1986 there were seven million players in Britain, with representatives of twenty five countries competing at international level. The World Professional Championship, held each spring at the Crucible Theatre in Sheffield, is one of the nation's great sporting occasions. It provides thrilling entertainment not only for the 980 or so spectators lucky enough to be in that ideal amphitheatre for the game, but for millions who watch on television.

From the 18.5 million who watched the climax of the epic Dennis Taylor v Steve Davis world final in 1985 to the one or two million faithful who will be in front of their sets for even the quietest afternoon session, televised snooker is the phenomenon of the age. Indeed snooker has become television's leading sport. BBC and ITV networked 383 hours coverage in 1985, plus some regional coverage, and the professional circuit is crammed with tournaments from one end of the season to the other.

The huge public appetite for snooker is anything but passive. People want to play, and hundreds of multi-table snooker centres have sprung up to cope with this demand. Standards of play are rising all the time, particularly among the young – and of both sexes. Some of the more precocious talents seem almost to have been born with a cue in their hand, so naturally do they fall into sound stance and true cueing.

Most are not so lucky. They either start with or develop technical faults which condemn them to a lifetime of mediocrity, however hard they try. They may be knowledgeable about shot selection, because they see so much good snooker on television, but what will be the right shot for someone who possesses a reliable cue action may prove suicidal for someone who does not. If you cannot deliver the cue through straight, you will never get anywhere with the game.

One of the prime values of this book is that an aspiring player can guide himself anew through basic techniques in the hope that by making a couple of changes he will transform his standard of play and therefore his enjoyment of the game. Beyond that, purposeful practice is as important to a snooker player as scales are to a pianist. The routines suggested are finely judged to develop the art of positional play – the secret of snooker. In particular the routine entitled 'The line-up', never before played through in sequence in an instructional book, is useful for players of all standards. Regardless of any limitations you may run up against in terms of potting ability, you will most certainly be able to improve your positional play so that you can consistently make substantial breaks when the balls are favourably placed. And remember that the top players, brilliantly as they may pot, tend to be rather keen to get on the next ball not just where they should pot it but where they can hardly miss it, even under the most severe pressure.

Finally, as an example of the game's infinite variety – and to prove that everything does not always go according to the book – I have contributed an analysis of one of the most remarkable breaks ever made, the 69 clearance by Alex Higgins against Jimmy White during the 1982 Embassy World Championship semi-final.

Clive Everton

Chapter 1 EQUIPMENT

To own a full-size snooker table can only be a dream for most of us, which means that by and large we have to take the 'hardware' of the game as we find it. That being so, it is advisable to gain experience of as wide a range of tables as possible – so that you can rapidly adjust to whatever conditions you encounter. But there is one vital exception to this fatalistic outlook: the cue. It is cheap enough to own your own cue, and if you are at all serious about raising your standard of play you should do so without delay.

The table

The standard full-size table measures approximately 12ft by 6ft. The identical nature of tables ends there. In the normal course of events you will find yourself playing on tables of excellent, mediocre and wretched quality. Some will be dead level and others disturbingly out of true. The cloth may be new, with good nap, or it may be badly worn, shiny even. The cushions may be lively or they may be 'dead'. The pockets may be big or small – not a reference to their actual size, which should be a uniform 3½ inches across, but to the amount of undercut they have. The greater the undercut, the more readily the pocket will accept the ball. This is particularly noticeable in the case of balls potted along a cushion. Temperature and humidity will affect the way any table plays.

Assuming you do not own your own table, all these factors are beyond your control. You will have to take the tables as you find them, and make

For all but a few, owning a full-size snooker table can only be a dream

what adjustments you can to the peculiarities of each. For that reason you should go out of your way to experience as wide a range of tables as possible. By doing so you will begin to find it easier and quicker to spot the good and bad points of an unfamiliar table. As for practice, try to use a table with 'big' pockets. That will make it easier for you to pot the ball, and it is only when you are able to pot with reasonable confidence that you can concentrate on positional play. If you learn to play on tight tables you will need to concern yourself so much simply with potting the next ball that

you will be unable to develop the rhythm and fluency necessary for break-building.

Smaller tables for the home are becoming increasingly popular, and their quality much improved. They are fun to play on, adequate for practising basic technique and ideal for introducing youngsters to the game. Steve Davis learned to play on a quarter-size table, which is as good a recommendation as any. Beyond a certain age, and a certain standard of skill, however, the real challenge of snooker can only be met by playing on a full-size table.

Preparing Sheffield's Crucible Theatre for the Embassy World Championships is a substantial task. The tables (two of them) must be winched in bit by bit to be installed in position. When the felt has been expertly fitted and ironed, the colour spots are then chalked with an 'X' (the physical spots found on club tables are not suitable for championship play, since the spotted colour is likely to come off with a 'kick'). Finally, all is in readiness for Dennis Taylor to put play in motion (above)

The balls

As with the tables, you will have to take the balls as you find them – which is generally very good these days. The original heavy ivory balls are a thing of the distant past. They were superseded before the Second World War by lighter Crystalate balls (made, gruesome as it may sound, from the crushed shin bones of cows). In recent years Crystalate balls have given way to Super Crystalate, which are entirely synthetic and ideally suited to the demands of the game. They are more lively than the Crystalate balls, which means they take spin more readily, thereby maximizing your opportunities for cue ball control – the key to snooker.

Super Crystalate balls are lively enough to take spin easily

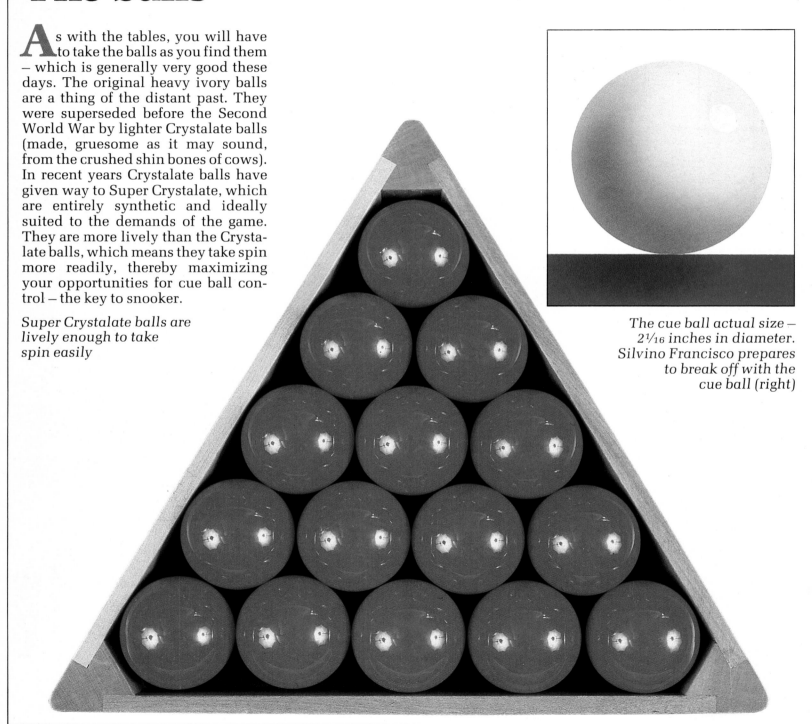

The cue ball actual size – 2¹⁄₁₆ inches in diameter. Silvino Francisco prepares to break off with the cue ball (right)

The cue

You are strongly advised to buy your own cue. No two cues play alike, so it is foolish to handicap yourself each time you play by having to come to terms with an unfamiliar one. It can be likened to playing the violin. Even a rank beginner would know better than to practise with bows picked at random.

The top professionals, with a single exception, guard their cues with their lives. The exception is the brilliant young Canadian, Kirk Stevens. He is not at all obsessional about his cue, regarding it as a bit of timber essential to his trade. The others shake their heads in disbelief at this eccentricity. For them, losing or damaging their cue is a horrific prospect. Once they have settled on a cue, early in their careers, they look forward hopeful-

ly to a lifelong partnership. Terry Griffiths reckons his to be about eighty years old. It is by conventional standards too thin and much too light, but that means nothing to him. It feels right, and therefore it is right – for him. John Spencer won his first two World Championships with a battered old cue that was warped. He claimed to feel lost with any other.

Starting from scratch, you will naturally choose a straight cue. The recommended weight is about 17 ounces, and it should taper down to a tip of about 10mm diameter. The butt should fit comfortably in the hand,

Terry Griffiths is attached to an ancient cue which is theoretically too thin and too light – but he would not be willingly parted from it

and the cue should feel balanced – reassuringly heavy in the shaft. The normal length is about 4ft 10in. The best cues are made of either ash or maple. Ash has a more visible grain, and Steve Davis for one prefers that because it enables him to hold the cue in the same position for each shot. Others prefer the more subdued grain of maple. Make sure there is a ferrule fitted to the tip end. This metal or plastic ring protects the end against splitting, and also against accidental damage when fitting and filing a new tip.

There are advantages to a two-piece cue. It is much more convenient to carry around, and it is less prone to warping. For the really serious player it has another advantage as well. By buying two identical tip sections,

Rex Williams chalks his cue in the proper manner – wiping the chalk lightly over the surface of the tip. Do not grind it in

and breaking both in, you have an immediate solution to any crisis caused by the tip coming off, or wearing down too much, during play. The reason most of the professionals use a one-piece cue is that they settled on their cue before the two-piece type was perfected. In the dreaded event of having to search out a new cue, most think they would turn to a two-piece.

Cue care

Because of its importance to your game, your cue needs the best of care. Do not lean it up against a wall, which encourages warping. Lay it flat if you are not using it for a few minutes. When you are not playing, always return it to its case (which can, of course, be leaned against a wall, although never leave it any place where it risks being knocked about). When storing the cue, avoid extremes of hot and cold (for example, in a car on a hot day or overnight in winter). Keep the cue clean with a damp cloth, and make sure your hands are clean before you play.

The leather tip is the only point of contact with the cue ball, and players are therefore extremely fussy about its condition. The tip should be firm yet resilient, to allow a certain amount of grip on the ball. You will soon develop a feel for the tip – you will know when it is right, and when it needs attention.

It is a good idea to learn to replace a worn tip yourself, a simple enough

Chalking the cue

Chalk is used to increase the grip of the tip on the cue ball. Green chalk is generally preferred to blue because it does not show up so much on the cue ball and the table. Do not grind it in. Simply wipe it a couple of times over the surface of the tip. Light and frequent are the watchwords. Follow the example of the pros, and get into the habit of chalking after almost every shot.

task and a satisfying one. File the bottom of the new tip and the end of the cue flat and clean. Then stick the tip on with either quick-drying or contact adhesive. When it is secure, file it into the classic dome-like shape, being careful always to file downwards so as not to risk dislodging the tip. When the tip becomes shiny through use it will fail to hold chalk. Tapping it gently with a file will roughen it up.

The rests

Such is the size of a snooker table that it is frequently impossible for even the tallest player to reach the cue ball – and it is important to reach the cue ball without overstretching. Several implements are designed to overcome this problem.

First there is the ordinary rest, which is sufficient to get you within comfortable reach of the cue ball most of the time. Sometimes it will not be long enough, in which case you must turn to the half butt, which is a long cue with a long rest (7½ft). And there are (mercifully rare) occasions when even the half butt is too short for your needs. The three-quarter butt is a nine-foot version of the half butt, a monstrous thing that no one would willingly use. Just as unpopular is the spider, a rest with a raised head which enables you to bridge at a distance over an intervening ball or balls near the cue ball. The cue extension is a recent and useful invention, and there are various types of manufacture. They fit snugly over the butt of the cue, and this allows a player to retain some of the feel of playing with his own cue – and of course tip – on certain shots that would otherwise require the use of the cumbersome and frequently ill-tipped half butt.

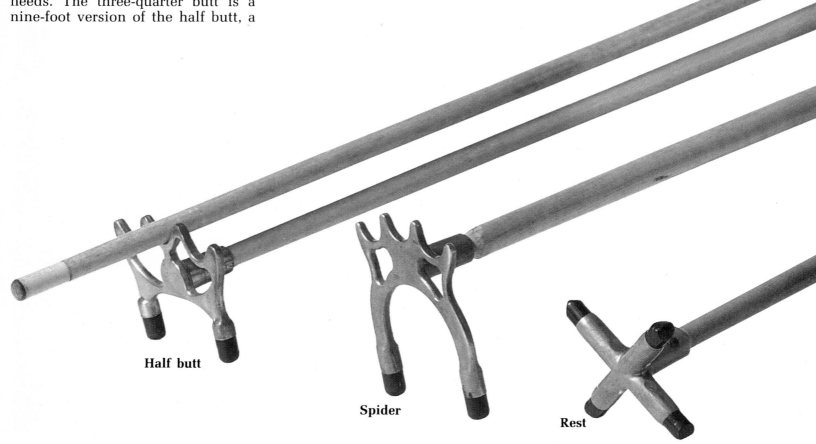

Half butt

Spider

Rest

The various rests are designed to enable you to reach an awkwardly-placed cue ball. The ordinary rest (top) is adequate for most situations where you are out of reach, but the longer half butt (right) is sometimes needed. The half butt rest can be used with a special cue extension (above) which fits over the butt of the cue. The spider (top right) allows you to bridge over an intervening ball

Chapter 2 CUE CONTROL

If you could possess only one chapter of this book, the one you are about to read would be of greater benefit to your game than all the others combined. That is because it deals with the fundamental skill of striking the cue ball properly – cue control. Ignore your cue action (because you think it suits you well enough) and you may as well forget the advanced aspects of the game. Improve it and the results will be immediate and continuous. You will be well on your way to achieving your goal – successful snooker.

Why the cue action is all-important

Anyone who has spent any time at all on a snooker table knows that it is easy enough to pot a red ball now and again. And if that pot leaves the cue ball well positioned on a colour, either by luck or intention, there is a good chance of knocking in the colour as well. In other words, even on the first occasion you picked up a cue it is virtually certain that you managed to pot a few reds, and quite likely that you managed the two ball sequence of red followed by colour, which is of course the cornerstone of the game. Those two balls represented a break – whether made by you in the course of your initiation or by Steve Davis on his way to another tournament victory.

If that is so, why is it a matter of common observation that the game is technically so difficult? Along with billiards it is probably the most technically difficult game ever devised. You know that, whether you are a novice, a casual club player or a good amateur. Millions who watch the game on television know that, including the large proportion who have never been near a table. The top professionals are never allowed to forget it.

The obvious strain the pros are under at critical moments in a vital frame is not caused by the TV lights and cameras, which most of them have lived with for so long that they seem normal furniture. Nor, as is frequently assumed, does it stem from the fact that the financial stakes are high. No one ever made a match-winning break with his mind on his bank balance. Nor is it simply that losing to a rival is a distasteful experience, to be avoided if at all possible. It feels better to win than to lose, but that universal emotion applies at club level as much as it does at the top. No, the principal reason for the strain, for the intense concentration of the players, and the palpable tension amongst the live audience and in front of millions of TV screens, is that the players are trying to do something very difficult. They know what to do and they know how to do it. All they have to do is strike the cue ball exactly right – a purely technical matter. If they do it they will succeed. If they do not they will fail.

The fundamental skill

Striking the cue ball exactly right is what snooker is all about. Striking it right not just now and again, which anyone can do, but again, and again and again.

That may sound like a gross over-simplification, but a moment's reflection will tell you that it is not. In order to achieve any desired result with the object ball (potting it being the most obvious one) and subsequently with the cue ball ('on' another pot or safe), you simply have to strike the cue ball at the correct point, on the correct line and with the correct strength. The correct line ensures the pot, while the other two factors determine the position on the table at which the cue ball will come to rest.

The skills involved in doing this are in varying degrees the finer points of snooker. They are the subject of the next chapter. Do not, however, even think of proceeding to that chapter until you have studied the present one. Until, indeed, you have absorbed the information here and incorporated it into your play. And that warning is directed at the club player of good standard as much as it is at the novice. The key to successful snooker is the cue action.

There is an exact parallel here with golf. It is plain to anyone that the action of the golf swing itself far outweighs any other aspect of the game. Choosing the right shot and the right club for it are simple matters, which

Snooker professionals have to become accustomed to performing under the glare of television lights – and the gaze of millions of armchair experts

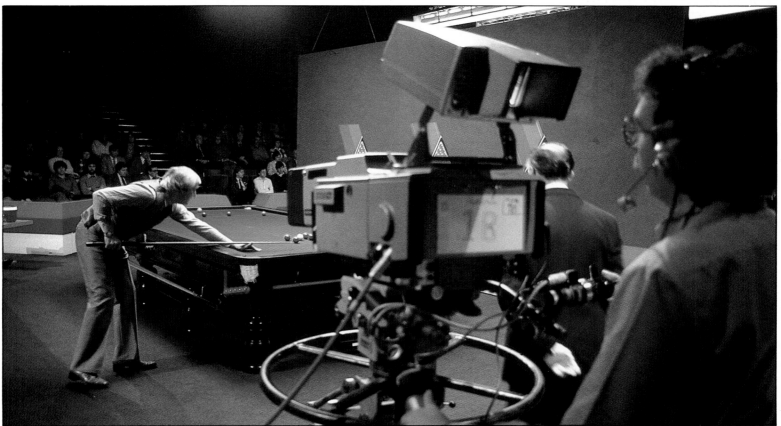

Why the cue action is all-important

is why when you watch Ballesteros on television you almost invariably know what he is trying to do. But the swing! That damnable swing! It is the curse of the Sunday golfer, and the bane of the professional's life. In both cases they practise it endlessly. They never doubt for a moment that if their swing is on song, the game will follow; that if it is not, all is in vain.

The key to success

For some curious reason, run-of-the-mill and even quite good snooker players do not have a similar obsession with their cueing action. They worry about potting angles and gaining position. They strive to gain cue ball control by the use of spin, so that they can move remorselessly from ball to ball, just as their idols do on television. They strive to turn their twenty breaks into forty breaks, and maybe in their wildest dreams they think the magical century break may one day come their way. Months and even years go by and they advance little beyond a rudimentary standard of play. Why? They understand the tactics of the game perfectly well — these may not be quite as simple as golf, but they are hardly a mystery even to those who content themselves with armchair play. They know when they have a good chance of making a pot and should therefore attempt it, and when they do not and should play a safety shot. With experience they learn positional play, which is obviously the key to the game, and scorn those who simply bang in a pot and hope for the best. They know all about attempting to lay and attempting to escape from snookers. Every so

often they rattle in a difficult long pot – not a fluke – that would almost force a smile from Jimmy White. And yet they cannot make those elusive big breaks, which alone would demonstrate real improvement. The twenty breaks do not become forty breaks, let alone centuries. In time they become resigned to the fact that they have reached their natural playing level.

They are wrong. They have come nowhere near it. All they need to do is to take a leaf out of the golfer's book. Let them look to their cueing action. And the cueing action begins with the stance.

When you can cue as consistently straight as Kirk Stevens, you will notice the results on the scoreboard

It is important to maintain a smooth action under difficult cueing circumstances – whether from an alarming angle like Jimmy White (above) or at full stretch like Steve Davis (left)

The stance

The reason the stance is so important is that at the moment of playing the shot the body should be absolutely still, with the exception of the right forearm (assuming you are right-handed). To be still you must be steady as a rock, and there is only one stance that will provide that steadiness, shot in and shot out.

The right *leg* should be roughly in line with the shot, with the right *foot* pointing to the right of that line at an angle of about sixty degrees. The left *foot* should be pointing roughly in line with the shot, and the distance between the feet should be twelve inches (more or less, depending upon the height and to some extent the

weight of the player). The left leg should be bent at the knee, which means the weight is forward, while the right leg must be ramrod straight. This is crucial. The right leg is your anchor and on no account should you move it. Take care that you do not involuntarily rise on your toes while you are making the shot. This is a common fault, easy to spot in other players and easy to cure by concentrating on it until keeping the leg still

Tony Knowles's stance, viewed from the right. Note how the left leg is bent at the knee, bringing the weight forward. The right leg is ramrod straight, anchoring the stance

becomes automatic.

You should find this position both comfortable and solid. If it is not comfortable, a minor adjustment of the feet will make it so. Stick your bottom out as far as it will go. This will make your back level rather than hunched. Guard against having your right leg too far back, as this will make your stance overextended. You may suspect that you make minor variations to this stance from one shot to another, but this is not a worry, as long as it remains essentially the same. As to solidity, that is easily demonstrated by adopting the stance and having someone give you a moderate push on the shoulder. You will

Three views of the grip, demonstrated by Silvino Francisco. The grip is relaxed, with the thumbs and first two fingers holding the cue. The most common fault is to grip too tightly, which reduces the freedom of the cue arm

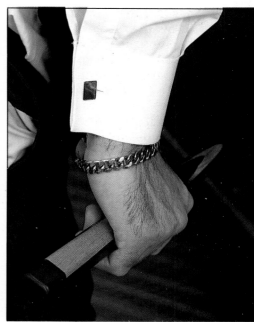

scarcely move. Then adopt any other conceivable stance (what you most commonly see is both knees bent, or, quite grotesque, both legs straight and splayed wide apart) and ask for a similar push. The difference will be apparent.

To reach difficult shots without using the rest it is sometimes impossible to adopt the basic stance. This is the exception that proves the rule. Go to any reasonable lengths to avoid using the rest, but beware of over-reaching. It is not enough for the cue tip just to be able to reach the cue ball. You must be able to make your preliminary addresses in a straight line, and also be able to follow through.

Steve Davis viewed from the left. Like Knowles, Davis is a tall man, yet he gets right down over the shot — with his bottom stuck out to ensure perfect balance

The grip

The grip is easy. Pick up the cue a few inches from the butt end as if you were going to use it as a club. Relax the tension in your hand. The cue should rest lightly, held just firmly enough to stop it sliding around. You will find that you are holding the cue with the thumb and first two fingers, while it is just resting on the back two fingers. The grip is so natural that there is only one common fault – gripping too tightly. This cuts down on the freedom of the cue arm, and it also prevents the natural slight squeeze of the fingers as you strike the ball. This little squeeze is automatic if the cue is held lightly to begin with, and it increases the 'feeling' of the shot.

The bridge

The bridge is important because it is one of the two contacts you have with the cue. And with the feet it forms a tripod, bolting you to the table. Lower your left hand on to the table and spread your fingers as wide as they will comfortably go. Grip the cloth with the finger pads, which will draw the fingers in slightly. Keep the fingers taut and unbent, and draw the thumb in tight to the forefinger. Cock the thumb as far as it will go, forming a V-shaped channel for the cue.

The first time you try to form a bridge it will probably be wobbly and uncomfortable. There will be a tendency to keep the fingers together rather than widely spread, and a temptation to let the thumb wander out, thereby forming the channel between thumb and forefinger rather than on them. Persevere until you get it right. Remember, the wider the base of the bridge, the more solid it will be. And keep the heel of your hand on the table – the more contact you have with the cloth the better.

Three views of the standard bridge, as demonstrated by Silvino Francisco. Note that the fingers are widely spread, with the finger pads gripping the cloth tightly and the thumb cocked against the forefinger to form a deep channel for the cue

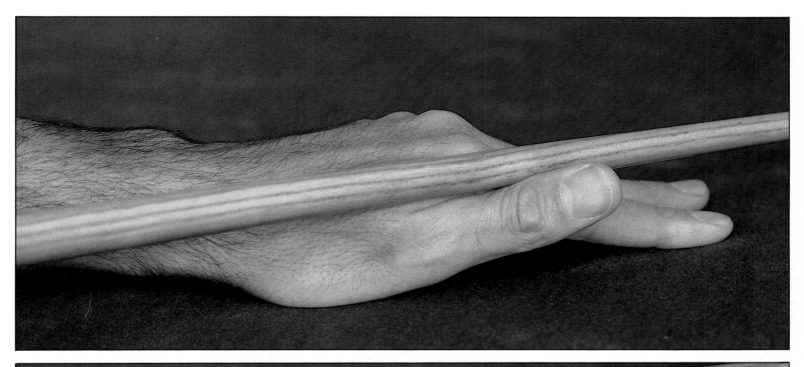

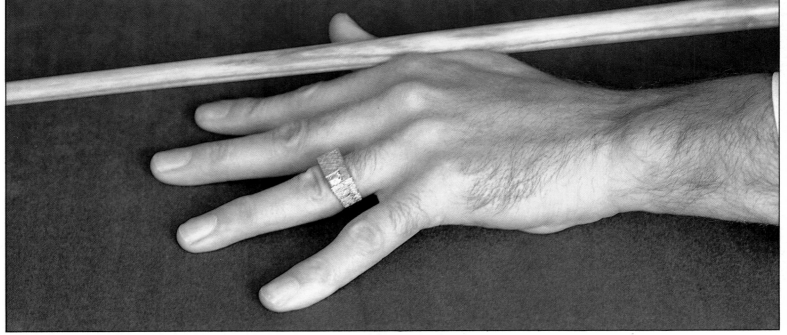

The bridge arm

The great Joe Davis, who virtually invented precision snooker as we know it today, has never been equalled as a theoretician of the game. His penetrating insights were the result of the most rigorous analysis of his own playing technique – not a bad model, since it was good enough to win him twenty consecutive world championships before he retired in 1947. Today's stars agree with virtually everything Davis ever said or wrote about the game – even when they neglect to put it into practice. On one point, though, most tend to disagree, however deferentially.

Extending the left arm

Davis was adamant that the left arm should be thrust out dead straight from the shoulder, to its maximum

Jimmy White's right forearm rests securely on the table in the approved manner. This gives the bridge and right shoulder complete stability

extension. In theory this makes sense, given the similarity between the action of sighting and cueing a ball and drawing a bow. In Davis's case, the theory and practice dovetailed nicely: he was a relatively small man (5ft 7in) and with his arm straight out he was at the optimum distance from the cue ball. Much taller players find that pushing the arm straight out leaves them a little too far from the cue ball. This not only feels awkward but it makes it virtually impossible

Cliff Thorburn is one of many taller players who ignore the great Joe Davis's instruction to thrust the bridge arm out completely straight. He feels more comfortable with the arm slightly bent. Steve Davis, taller than Thorburn, bends his even more, and with results like theirs who is to quarrel?

to follow through properly. The cue should be accelerating to the maximum speed required for the particular shot as it goes *through* the cue ball. You do not want the cue power to be spent by the time the cue actually reaches the cue ball. Tall players find it more comfortable to be slightly more compact on the table, and so they bend the left arm slightly. Steve Davis, who is well over six feet tall, does this to a noticeable extent. Do whichever suits you, bearing in mind that feeling comfortable on the table is a vital consideration and that the whole of the forearm must rest securely on the table.

Rex Williams (left) addresses the ball in a classic, easy manner, one of the reasons he has long been a player of the highest class. Joe Johnson (above) thrusts the arm out straight, on the way to winning the 1986 world title

The cue arm

The emphasis on stance, bridge and bridge arm is in a sense only the means to an end. The end is the cue action itself. Get the cue action right, consistently right, and you are on your way to playing good snooker.

In describing the correct cue action, Joe Davis likened it to the movement of a piston. The cue is the piston, the wrist and forearm the connecting rods. This mechanical image is particularly appropriate because it is easily grasped, and it draws attention to the fact that as far as humanly possible the cue action should be mechanical. Like a well-oiled machine, the cue arm should perform the same motion over and over again without any variation.

Adopt the correct stance and form the bridge. Slot the cue into the 'V' of the bridge and lean forward until the cue just brushes your chin beneath your nose. If you are holding the cue a few inches from the butt end, this should bring your right forearm into a vertical position. Consider the elbow as a hinge, from which the forearm will swing easily back and forth, like a pendulum. The vertical position of the forearm at rest is important because it means that the sequence of backswing, strike and follow-through can be accomplished while keeping the cue almost completely horizontal. That is the goal, a horizontal cue action. If the forearm at rest is behind vertical (as it would be if you held the cue at the butt end), the cue will tend to come through with a scooping action. If the forearm at rest is in front of vertical, the cue will tend

to lift off the bridge on the shot and follow through.

Ideally, there should be a straight line running from the raised right elbow to the tip of the cue. That is the perfect alignment: arm, cue and line of shot as one. Some players fall into it naturally. John Spencer used invariably to be cited as having perfect alignment. In still-life line-up he still does, but his slide down the rankings in recent years is attributable ultimately to the fact that he has lost his straightness of cue action in motion. Television has often shown him not bringing the cue back in a straight line, so obviously he is not bringing it through straight. Steve Davis, on the other hand, was always pretty straight, but he has kept working at it over the years, trying to make – and keep – it straighter still. With a single exception, all the top players

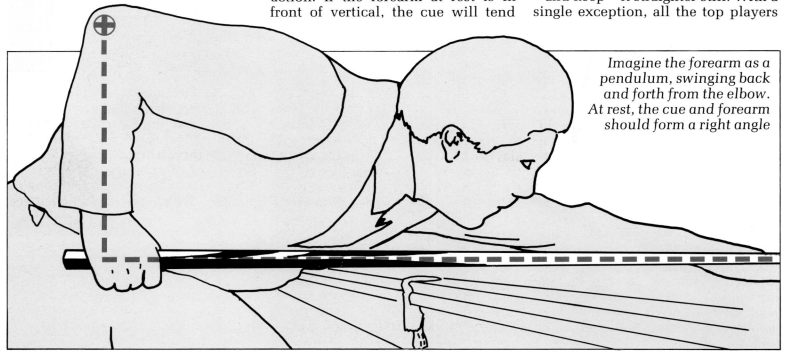

Imagine the forearm as a pendulum, swinging back and forth from the elbow. At rest, the cue and forearm should form a right angle

John Spencer (above left) cueing with perfect alignment, in contrast to Ray Reardon (above), whose elbow juts out noticeably. Despite this technical fault (the result of a childhood injury) Reardon still brings the cue through straight — which is what really matters

demonstrate nearly true alignment. The exception is six-times world champion Ray Reardon. His right elbow juts out alarmingly, which means that his wrist is turned outward as well. This is because Reardon broke his shoulder as a child, and he cannot cue any other way. He insists that the eccentric cue action forced upon him by necessity has never impaired his game, and, with a record like his, who is to argue? All it really proves, however, is that great talent and application can compensate for technical frailty. You will play better snooker if you model your cue action on John Spencer's rather than Ray Reardon's (unless you can claim an identical childhood injury!).

Having said that, beware of trying to imitate the television stars in a slavish manner. By all means watch them critically. Try to recognize the strengths and weaknesses in their techniques, and, where you can, apply your observations to your own technique. However, remember that you are an individual, as each of them is, and just as their styles vary one from the other, so must yours be individual. It is the general principles of sound technique that you must acquire, not a copycat image of your favourite player.

Lining up the shot

As well as the piston analogy, Joe Davis likened the cue action to that of a rifle. The 'V' of the bridge is the sight, and what you are trying to do is line up the target (the object ball) along the cue and through that sight. Having done that, you effectively push the cue through the bridge along the sight line (propelling the cue ball straight along that sight line to the object ball). Again, it is an apt image, and it explains why there is so much emphasis placed on complete stillness during the shot. Nothing must move except the trigger finger when you fire a rifle. Nothing must move except the right forearm when you play a shot. It also explains why the head must be right down on the cue, the eyes looking directly along the line of shot.

Here again there are exceptions (notably, Joe Davis himself). If your eyes are of roughly equal strength, it will be natural to use both of them in sighting the shot. The cue will be brushing the centre of your chin. But if one eye is significantly stronger than the other, you will necessarily favour that eye. Joe Davis had a weak right eye, and he played with the cue running directly beneath his left eye. So does Rex Williams. In a less pronounced way, many players slightly favour one eye, either by a fractional tilt of the head or a minor adjustment of the stance. The most extreme example of all is provided by Graham Miles; not only is he left-eyed, but he has an imposing chin. How do you get right down on the ball when you have such a chin getting in the way? Well, Miles has developed a method of sighting that nearly defies

belief. The cue runs beneath his left ear and brushes his left cheek. If he moved it any further out he would be playing on the next table! Try that yourself and you may wonder how Miles can even hit the cue ball, let alone play snooker of the quality that brought him two Pot Black championships in the early 1970s (not to mention a couple of 147 breaks). It is another example of the triumph of talent over technique.

Steve Davis takes deadly aim, as though down the barrel of a rifle. His alignment could not be more perfectly straight, from elbow to cue tip, with the cue brushing his chin directly beneath his nose

Not all snooker players are able to sight with both eyes because one of their eyes is significantly weaker than the other. Commonly it is the right eye that is the weaker, and such players therefore sight with the left eye – running the cue beneath it. Joe Davis (left) was notoriously left-eyed, which did not stop him from achieving a record that even his illustrious namesake Steve will have trouble equalling – twenty consecutive world championships. Willie Thorne (below left) is equally left-eyed, while John Parrott sights down the cue dead centre

The cueing action

Assume that you have surveyed the table, selected your shot and determined the potting angle. You are perfectly clear in your mind about your intentions. (This, incidentally, is of the utmost importance. Never begin to address the cue ball until you are sure of the shot you are going to play.) Get into cueing position in line with the shot, with the bridge formed some nine to twelve inches from the cue ball, as feels right. When you are comfortable and confident that you are in the correct position, start addressing the cue ball as a golfer does a golf ball, with several approaches. The purpose of this feathering is threefold. It allows you to check that you are cueing straight and it builds rhythm and it assists concentration. Ignore the example of Jimmy White (unless you happen to share his natural genius). First-time sighting and the minimum of preparation work for him, but then when White is in full flood he makes every aspect of the game look ridiculously easy. You know better.

At the same time, there is no point in overdoing these preliminaries, as some players do on even the simplest of pots. Here again the rifle analogy is useful. Just as the marksman is not likely to make his best shot by taking one quick glance down the sight and firing, he is also not going to make it by staring interminably down the sight while trying to hold his body motionless. The longer he waits, the greater the chance of involuntary movement.

Finally, while you are feathering keep your body and head absolutely still. There is nothing whatever to be said for the way Alex Higgins bobs around while he is addressing the ball, all those jerky, twitchy mannerisms, the staccato feathering, that whole collection of eccentricities so hilariously parodied by John Virgo. Higgins is prodigiously gifted, and there may never be anyone to match him when it comes to conveying the sheer thrill of watching genius on the loose. But his style is not for the coaching manual.

Ignore the pocket

While feathering, you should keep checking that your cueing is straight, and that the cue is directed at the point on the cue ball that you want to hit. Meanwhile, your eyes will be flickering back and forth between cue ball and object ball, or, rather, between cue ball and the part of the object ball you intend to hit. Remember, you have determined the angle you need on the object ball before getting down over the shot, so you have nothing whatever to think about except hitting the object ball at the point needed to achieve that angle. The pocket by this stage is irrelevant, and you should resist the temptation to look at it. What good is looking at it anyway? It has hardly moved since you selected the angle. If you have got the angle right, and play the shot as you intend, you will make the pot. If you have got the angle wrong you will miss it. If while you are cueing a doubt creeps into your mind about the angle, you must stop. Stop completely that is, not simply change the line of the shot while remaining in the cueing position. Stand up, look at the balls for as long as you need to judge the angle again, and then repeat the cueing sequence. The point is, however, that once you are down on the shot the pocket is a useless distraction. You have as much as you can handle in making sure that you strike the cue ball where you want to strike it, and that in doing so you send it in a straight line to the part of the object ball at which you are aiming.

When you sense that the moment has come to play the shot, you will begin the final backswing. It should be a somewhat shorter backswing than you have been using while feathering, where you were building up your rhythm. The rhythm is now there, and when you come to strike the cue ball you want no more backswing than is necessary to make a clean, flowing stroke of the strength required. An exaggerated backswing means that the cue will travel further than it needs to, and the further it travels the more likely it is to go off line. The further it travels the harder it is to keep the cue on the horizontal. Both opinion and practice vary on the extent of the backswing, but for a shot of normal strength five or six inches should be about right.

As you begin that final backswing your eyes should be on the cue ball, checking for the last time that you are going to strike it where you intend. As the backswing progresses – at an unhurried pace – your eyes should travel from the cue ball to the object ball. And there they should stay, throughout the shot. Your cue arm, cue and eyes are all now together on the line of the shot, and by fixing your eyes on the end of that line you pretty

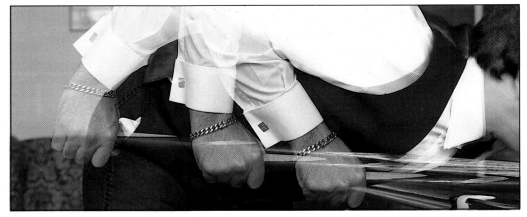

well guarantee that the cue will come through on that line. The cue automatically follows the eye if you are cueing straight.

As you complete that final backswing, eyes now fixed unwaveringly on the object ball, pause for the briefest of moments. Do not overdo it — little more than a hesitation. Precisely why this pause is important is not completely clear. Presumably it gives you a final fraction of a second to secure your sight on the object ball, and perhaps it provides a sort of freeze-frame on the whole of the body, bringing everything into unison for the moment of striking. Top golfers provide an analogy. The most fluent swings bring the club smoothly back to a slight pause at the top of the backswing before the club comes down and through. Whatever the reason, there is no disputing its importance in the cueing sequence, although here again you will observe marked differences between the top players. Doug Mountjoy scarcely seems to pause at all (although he does, just), whereas Steve Davis almost allows you to draw in your breath in anticipation.

Silvino Francisco demonstrates the three stages of the cueing sequence (from the top): the rest position, the backswing and pause position, and the follow-through position. The freeze-action photograph shows the complete action

Striking the cue ball

The slight pause on the final back-swing, eyes on the part of the object ball you are aiming to hit, and now strike cleanly through the cue ball. Do not lift your head or shift your gaze. Keep looking at the object ball as the cue ball makes its journey. Keep looking at it as the cue ball collides with it. Keep looking at it, or, rather, at the spot where it was, *after* it has disappeared in the direction of the pocket. Keep your eyes on that spot until you hear the satisfying clunk as it hits the bottom of the pocket.

That may sound excessive, since once the cue ball is on its way everything is in the lap of the gods. What earthly difference can it make if you watch it approach the object ball, and then watch the object ball on its way to the pocket? After all, you are keenly interested in the course of the shot, so why not gratify your curiosity? This is the reason. In all games that involve striking a ball, from golf to cricket, from tennis to football, the cardinal sin is to take your eye off the ball before striking. There is an almost irresistible urge to do just that, because once you are committed to making the shot, once you are actually in the throes of doing it, your mind leaps forward to the outcome. And as your mind leaps so do your eyes and head. The only way you can guarantee that you do not take your eyes off the ball *before* striking it is to force yourself to keep them on the ball, or where the ball was, *after* striking it. Hence the way the golfer struggles against nature to keep his head down throughout the swing.

It is the same with snooker. You must discipline yourself to keep the

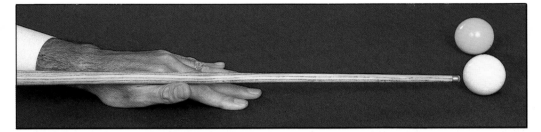

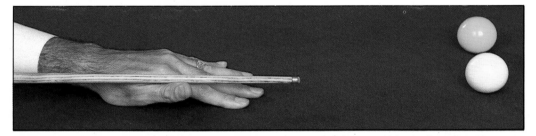

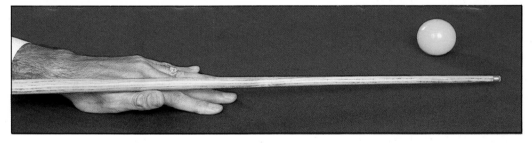

head steady (which means keeping the eyes steady, for the head will follow the eyes) for a measurable time after you have struck the cue ball. If you do not do that you will be in grave danger of moving your head before you have struck the cue ball. When that happens, and it will almost certainly be at critical moments when you are most keyed up, you will have destroyed the very basis of the cue action. Marvel if you like at the way Higgins seems to break this rule with impunity – the head shooting up as he cracks in some fiendishly difficult long pot. But watch Steve Davis, and follow his example.

The striking action, showing (top to bottom) the final address, final backswing and pause, and follow-through

Follow-through and stop

Up to and including the pause, each element in the cue action can be examined and practised in isolation. But the strike, follow-through and stop cannot. They are inextricably linked in the one movement. Fortunately, the cue action is a natural one in the sense that the follow-through and the stop follow automatically from a clean strike.

A clean strike is not a push, much less a slash, however powerfully the stroke is played. It is not even a swing, although it should be smooth and flowing. It is best described as a punch, and as with a punch the action continues beyond the point of impact. The extent of the follow-through (and therefore the point at which the cue stops) will depend on the strength of the shot and the intended course of the cue ball following it. However, every shot, including screw, requires follow-through. Experience alone will guide you here, and it is fair to say that every good player follows through as the shot and the peculiarities of his own cue action dictate, quite automatically.

Hitting the cue ball straight

Everything to this point has been devoted to the sole end of hitting the cue ball in a straight line. Apart from the rare occasion on which you want to swerve the cue ball, hitting the cue ball straight is an essential part of every successful shot. There is an easy way to check whether you are cueing straight. On an empty table, play the cue ball from the brown spot, over the blue, pink and black spots, hard enough to bring the cue ball off the top cushion and back down the table. Because there is no object ball to focus on, treat the blue spot as the object ball during the shot. You should have no difficulty in running the cue ball over the spots on the outward journey, but what happens on the way back? If you are cueing dead straight, and not imparting any unintentional side-spin to the cue ball, it will come back near enough over the spots. It is a foolproof test, and many professional players start every serious practice session with it. When you can do it consistently with a medium strength shot, gradually increase the pace. It gets more diffi-

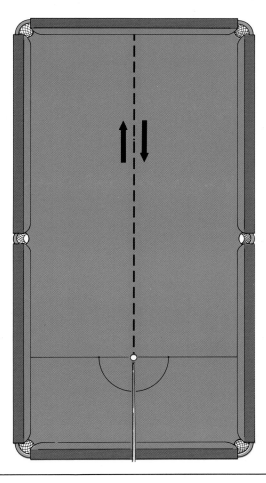

cult as the pace increases, and with a full power shot you will never consistently be closer than a couple of inches from the brown spot on the return. The moral of this is that you should never hit the cue ball harder than necessary to achieve a desired result. The harder you strike it the greater the risk of inaccurate cueing.

Playing the cue ball up and down the spots will reveal basic cueing faults. If you cue straight, without unintentional side-spin, the cue ball will pass over the blue, pink and black spots, and then return on the same line

Chapter 3 CUE BALL CONTROL

It is obvious even to the most casual observer that controlling the cue ball is what the game of snooker is all about. On the one hand, cue ball control is the essential ingredient of accurate potting (and without accurate potting, positional play is a complete waste of time). On the other, cue ball control alone makes positional play possible (and to attempt potting without positional consideration is to adopt a trivial, highly unrewarding approach to the game). Armed with a reliable cue action, you are now ready to get to grips with the genuine skills of snooker and play to win.

The art of potting

Once you can strike the cue ball in a straight line you are ready to tackle potting. Good potting is essential, for the obvious reason that it is the only feasible way of putting together enough points to win a frame. That is not to deny the importance of snookering your opponent under the right circumstances, but points gained by laying successful snookers can hardly build a winning score. You can only build this by amassing breaks.

Break-building is a combination of accurate potting and sound positional play. Miss the pot, however, and the effort to secure good position for the following shot is wasted. In fact it can easily rebound against you. Suppose you are attempting to pot a colour and secure position on the only available red. If you miss the pot but succeed in gaining position on the red your opponent will be very pleased. In such a situation, and it is a common one, getting your shot half right is worse than fluffing it altogether.

It is often said that potting ability is largely innate, that a good potter

Jimmy White is often described as the most gifted potter in the game. He can make it look ridiculously easy

has 'a good eye', a natural ability to size up angles – in a word, flair. Consequently, mediocre potters become resigned to their limitations in this respect. They sigh wistfully as they watch the good potter, the 'born' potter, and reflect on the unfairness of life. They pin their hopes on safety play, but in their hearts they know that the better potter almost always wins, and deservedly so. They are beaten before they begin.

This is largely bunk. Of course it is true that Jimmy White is a born potter, in the sense that he is uncannily gifted at this aspect of the game. However, you are unlikely to be competing against Jimmy White. Good potting is an acquired skill, even for White. You do not need 'a good eye' as you do for games with a moving ball, where you have to be able to gauge speed and flight quickly and accurately – almost instinctively. Snooker is a static game, like golf and bowls. As such, it is almost completely dependent upon technique. That is why so much emphasis is placed on cue action. Anyone who pots consistently well has a good cue action. Whether that good cue action was acquired by happy accident, or

Alex Higgins (above) has captivated an entire generation of fans with his spectacular potting, while Stephen Hendry (right) is a potting prodigy

by diligent practice, is immaterial – it is there, on open display. Conversely, no matter how frustratingly inept your potting may be at the moment, if you acquire a good cue action your potting must improve. As it improves, it will make sense for you to turn your attention to the more interesting and rewarding aspects of the game.

Plain ball potting

A plain ball shot is one in which you strike the cue ball dead centre. It is in contrast to spin shots of all descriptions – stun, screw, topspin, side, or side in conjunction with one of the others. Novices can hardly wait to attempt these advanced shots, particularly so in these days of televised snooker. The commentators scatter the terms around like confetti, making it pretty apparent that stun, screw and the rest play an enormous part in the game. They do indeed, but there is a snag. When the commentator coolly informs you that Cliff Thorburn is going to play a simple stun on the red, which will bring him nicely on to the black, he neglects to point out a banal truth. Thorburn could not possibly pot the red using stun (the killing of forward move-

ment achieved by striking the cue ball somewhat below centre) unless he could pot it with a plain ball shot. He is using stun to gain position for the next shot (to get nicely on to the black), not because he has a fondness for stun. It follows from this that until you come to terms with plain ball potting you are wasting your time even thinking about the mysteries of spin.

Consider first the matter of potting in a straight line, since this avoids the problem of choosing the correct angle. If the cue ball and object ball are in a direct line with the pocket,

The plain ball shot involves striking the cue ball dead centre.
Learn to do that consistently before attempting spin

it is simply a matter of striking the object ball full face. This shot cruelly exposes flaws in basic technique, and is therefore the natural place to start.

Take the diagonal line between corner pockets and place the cue ball on the baulk line where the diagonal crosses it. Place the object ball a foot or so up the table, also on the diagonal. You now have a straight pot into the corner pocket. In theory, you should be able to make the pot consistently. In practice, you cannot – consistently. Why? The possible reasons for failure are severely limited. Either you sighted wrongly or struck the cue ball wrongly. If the latter, you must either have lined yourself up incorrectly for the shot (which should have been through the centre of the cue ball) or failed to

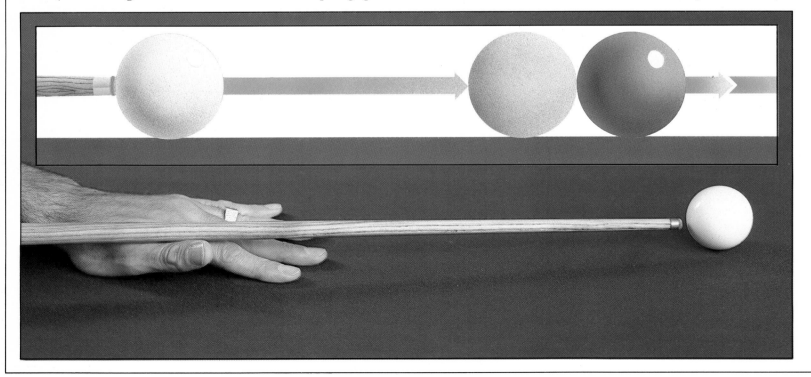

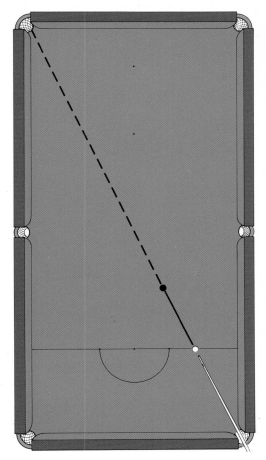

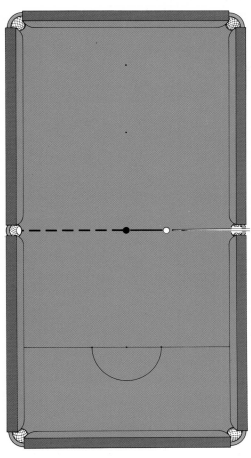

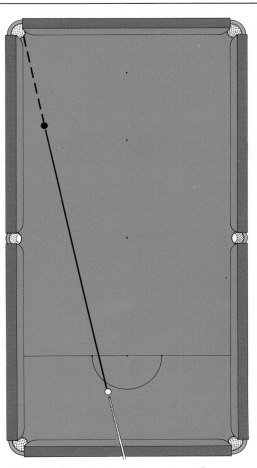

Practise this straight pot into the top pocket – plain ball

This straight pot is within reach of the absolute beginner

A straight pot that is eminently missable by anyone

deliver the cue in a straight line. As usual, you have been let down by your technique.

The more grooved your cue action becomes, the more you will succeed with straight pots, especially over distance, which magnifies the effect of any inaccuracy. Straight pots, more than any others, highlight the difficulty posed by distance. With the blue on its spot and the cue ball a few inches away, in direct line with the middle pockets, you have a pot well within reach of the complete novice. With the cue ball in the baulk area and the object ball three-quarters of the way up table, in direct line with a corner pocket, you have a pot that even a world champion would regard as no certainty.

The plain ball shot (full ball) as it appears to the player – aiming dead centre on the cue ball

Potting at an angle

The angled potting attempt is far and away the most common shot in snooker. Skill or lack of it in this department is generally decisive in the outcome of any contest. Therefore, any real improvement here is bound to be reflected in your results. What is the secret of potting at an angle?

There is no secret. Indeed such theories as there are on the subject are more of a hindrance than a help. There is a widespread assumption that when snooker balls collide, they are deflected along lines that are predictable by the laws of geometry and basic physics. The idea that snooker is in this sense purely geometrical is a fallacy, but an understandable one. The route taken by the balls following collision is indeed *roughly* in line with geometry. But it is not *exactly* geometrical, which means that if you search for the geometrical potting angle you will miss the true potting angle.

The difference between the two angles is easier to demonstrate than it is to explain. The geometrical angle would be achieved by striking the object ball at a point diametrically opposite the pocket. In other words, if at the point of contact between the cue ball and the object ball the two are lined up for the pocket (like a plant), according to the geometrical principle the object ball should go to the pocket. It should behave as it would have behaved had you played a dead straight pot from directly behind the object ball, because you are striking it at exactly the same point. In practice, if the object ball is within twelve inches or so of the

pocket, the geometrical angle will see you home. At double that distance, where the margin of error is less, it will invariably let you down. At eight feet it will lead you astray to an embarrassing degree. The shot will be too thick, because the actual angle of deflection will be less than geometry would have it. The difference between the geometrical and true potting angle is small, but then the difference between making and barely missing a pot is a small one. It is the consequences that loom large.

An explanation of this demonstrable fact must come down to the resistance, or friction, between the balls and the cloth. But the explanation is unimportant. You must accept that for all shots other than straight or nearly straight ones, the geometrical angle is only a near guide to the true potting angle. You must find the true potting angle by experiment, and then commit it to memory.

Potting from memory

Potting angles are chiefly a matter of memory. When good potters say that they know potting angles instinctively, what they really mean is that any potting situation looks familiar to them, and they know from memory how to pot from that particular angle.

This may sound implausible, since between a dead straight contact and the finest of cuts there must be an infinite number of possible angles. With the balls spread haphazardly around the table, never the same from one game to the next, how can memory tell you the precise potting angle? Mercifully, snooker has been

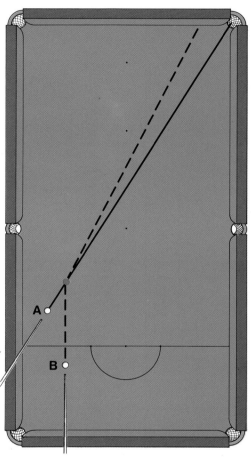

If the geometrical and potting angles were the same, B would result in a pot, like A. In fact, the geometrical angle is too thick and B misses

designed for mortals. Potting may strike you as fiendishly difficult, but it need not be truly precise. A snooker ball is two-and-one-sixteenth inches in diameter. The pocket is three-and-a-half inches across at the fall of the slate, which means that it is a little over one-and-a-half widths of the ball. This provides a decent margin of error to work within, and it means

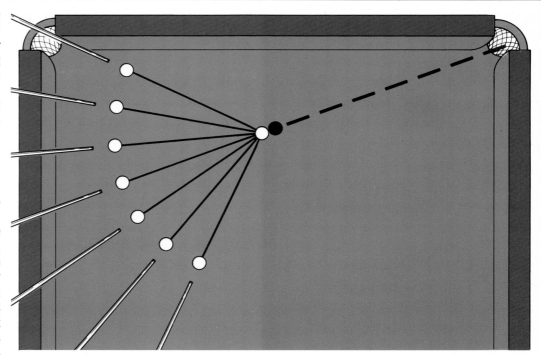

An excellent practice routine for developing potting skill around the black spot. Simply work your way round the top of the table potting the black from its spot — from one quarter-ball angle to the other. Practise it from both sides so as not to develop a preference

that you need not worry about an infinite number of potting angles.

In practice, potting angles are reassuringly few. There is full ball, which is no angle at all, and there is fine cut, which is as close to ninety degrees as you can manage. (You will have noticed that the professionals sail so close to the wind on the finest cuts that not infrequently they miss the object ball.) Between these extremes are three distinct potting angles: three-quarter ball, half-ball, and quarter-ball.

For the three-quarter ball angle an imaginary line through the centre of the cue ball would run midway between the centre and the outside edge of the object ball (three-quarters of the object ball is 'covered' at impact). For the half-ball angle, this imaginary line would barely brush the outside edge of the object ball (half the object ball is 'covered'). For the quarter-ball angle it would miss the edge of the object ball by one-quarter its width (one-quarter of the object ball is 'covered').

These five angles, from full ball to fine cut, are all you have to burden yourself with. Admittedly, you will find yourself making slight modifications to them as experience (and memory) dictate. A half-ball angle may be a shade more than half-ball or a shade less, but it is still basically a half-ball angle. If you can recognize it as such, you are on your way to potting it. The really critical judgment is to identify the basic potting angle from any position on the table. A half-ball angle is a half-ball angle wherever it crops up. This means that you should be able to overcome irrational fears about particular potting situations. If you see it correctly as a half-ball pot, and play it that way, you will make the pot whether it is from left to right, right to left, into a middle pocket, into a corner pocket, off the black spot or from the 'D'.

It follows from this that there is no short cut, no magic formula for consistent potting — which must be your goal. You must learn to recognize potting angles by trial and error, both in practice and during play. If you persistently miss a particular type of shot, stick with it until you find the right angle. Once you have found it, commit it to memory. And so on to the next. It is a matter of conscious application, of carefully noting what happens when you miss a pot and gaining from the experience, rather than just writing it off.

Learning the angles

Any systematic potting practice is good for locating and memorizing potting angles. Here is one that is not only helpful generally, but specifically geared to improving your score in the next frame you play.

Potting the black is your most eagerly awaited opportunity. To the beginner, and not just the beginner, a black ball pot seems more daunting than an identical red ball pot because the stakes are in pure scoring terms seven times as high. To cure this costly inhibition, practise potting the black off its spot. As the level at which you play snooker improves, potting the black off its spot becomes an increasingly important shot. In the professional game it is *the* dominant shot because of its pivotal role in most break-building. Therefore the sooner you get used to potting it routinely the better.

Spot the black and place the cue ball so as to leave yourself a quarter-ball pot. Then move the cue ball to the half-ball angle, then the three-quarter, the full, then on to the other three-quarter ball angle, the half, and the quarter. Practise these shots (into both top pockets, so as not to develop a preference) until you feel confident that the angles are locked permanently in your memory. You may never feel confident of making these shots with the clinical ease that the professionals demonstrate, but you will recognize them for what they are. Knowing how to make a particular pot is not the same thing as making it, but it more than somewhat increases your chances.

The world of spin

The plain ball shot is fine for potting, but severely limited for positional play. The reason it is so limited is that the cue ball will be deflected off the object ball on the precise angle predetermined by the potting angle. Since you have no choice about the potting angle, you have no control over the cue ball's leaving angle. It will go where it will go. At least it will do so in terms of direction. You can control the strength, or weight of the shot, and that will determine the distance along the line of direction that the cue ball will travel. However, it is notoriously difficult to control the cue ball with sufficient accuracy using weight alone. Even if you could do so, you would still find your choice of position dictated by that invariable line of departure. With every shot you would be on tramlines for the next.

Spin spells success

Only by breaking free of those tramlines does serious break-building become a realistic possibility. The best potter in the world would be lucky to make a break of forty using plain ball shots alone, and that only under rarely favourable circumstances. He would feel himself in chains. Spin is the great liberator.

What spin does – any kind of spin – is alter the course of the cue ball following its collision with the object ball. Topspin and backspin do so immediately. Side-spin (referred to simply as side) takes effect when the cue ball hits a cushion. Side can be used in conjunction with either topspin or backspin.

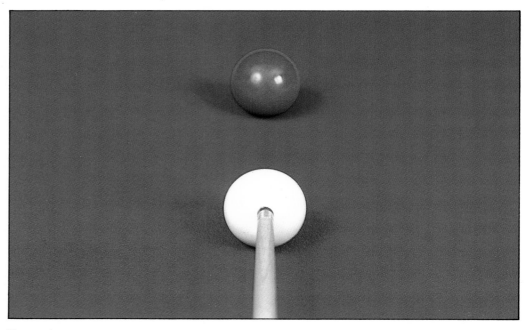

Topspin

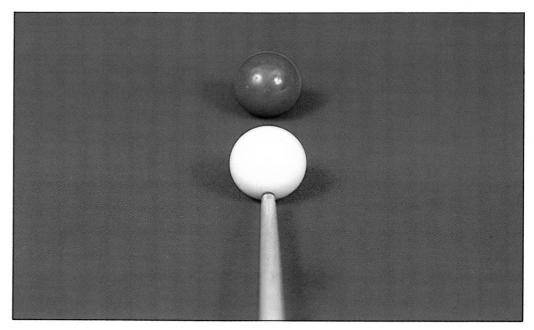

Backspin

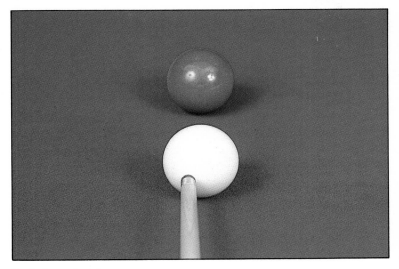

Left-hand side

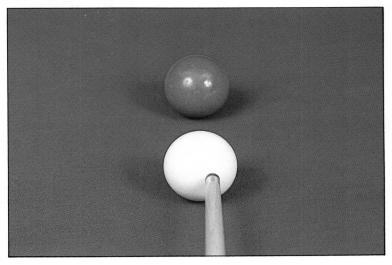

Right-hand side

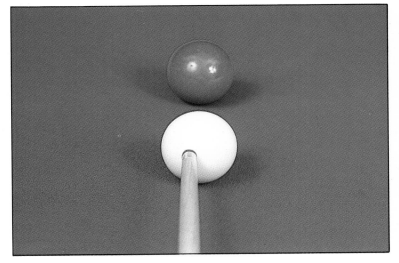

Left-hand side topspin

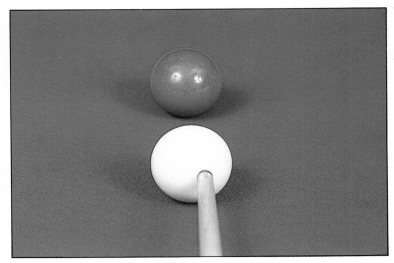

Right-hand side topspin

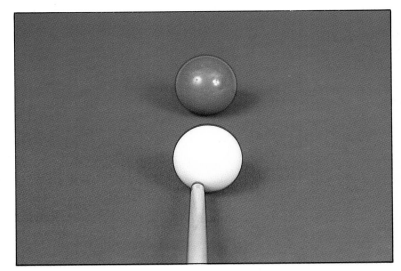

Left-hand side backspin

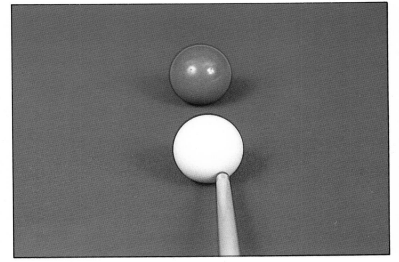

Right-hand side backspin

Topspin

If you strike the cue ball above centre you impart topspin. The higher you strike it the greater the topspin, always providing that the cue tip follows through nicely to accentuate the spinning action. The effect of topspin is to assist the ball's forward motion, so that when it strikes the object ball it runs through further than it would do with a plain ball shot. You have probably hit the odd shot with accidental topspin – and with spectacularly awful consequences. You have slammed in an easy straight pot, because slamming it in feels so good, and then watched in horror as the cue ball leapt in pursuit of the object ball, to be happily reunited in the bottom of the pocket. That was topspin, caused in this case by one or more of the familiar deadly sins – jerking the head or coming through with a scooping action. Topspin used deliberately, often in conjunction with side, is a valuable addition to your repertoire of shots. When using it, raise your bridge slightly so as to keep the cue action horizontal. Beware of aiming too high

on the cue ball – it is easy to miscue. The tip of the cue should be travelling at its fastest as it strikes and goes through the cue ball. This is how maximum power and control can be obtained without strain.

The effect of topspin is to accentuate the spinning action of the cue ball, so that it runs through further after contacting the object ball. When applying topspin, avoid striking too high, which would result in a miscue

Backspin

The repertoire of backspin strokes – screw, stun and drag – lie at the heart of snooker. If you strike the cue ball below centre you impart backspin. The lower you strike it the greater the backspin, provided that you follow through correctly. Backspin works against the ball's natural forward motion. The ball is travelling forward, towards the object ball, but it itself is spinning backwards all the time. Upon impact, the backspin counteracts the cue ball's natural forward momentum. The actual effect this has on the cue ball depends upon a combination of factors, and it is the effect that gives rise to the description of the shot – as a screw shot, a deep screw shot, a stun shot and so forth.

The language of backspin

It is important to understand the language of backspin here and now, because for the remainder of this book the various terms will be used without further explanation. It is common even for good players to get into a muddle when describing variations of backspin, and if you are confused by the words you will most surely be misled by the information. The difficulty is caused by the use of the word screw in two distinct senses. On the one hand there is screw as in applying screw to the cue ball, or screwing the cue ball. In that sense, screw is used to describe the technique of applying any degree of backspin, whatever the outcome. To play most stun shots or a drag shot you employ screw (backspin). The exception to this is where the cue ball and object ball are very close together, when stun will be achieved by central

The effect of backspin is to counter the cue ball's forward motion so that it will not run through in the normal manner after impact

striking or even slightly above centre. Typical stun shots and drag shots are simply two results of employing screw. On the other hand, there is the screw shot itself. The screw shot, like the stun and drag shots, is the particular result of the application of screw. More or less screw (backspin), in combination with other factors, will result in a screw shot, a stun shot or a drag shot.

The other factors in the equation are the distance between the cue ball and the object ball and the speed of the cue ball. However much or little screw you apply to the cue ball, the backspin is at its maximum as the ball leaves the tip of the cue. It wears off continuously as the cue ball travels to the object ball. Therefore, the further the cue ball has to travel, and the longer it takes to get there, the smaller the proportion of the original backspin still active upon contact. In consequence, a given amount of screw played over a short distance will have a much greater screwing effect than it will played over a long distance. So will a given amount of screw played with pace rather than gently. Hence, the amount of screw that it takes to stop the cue ball dead upon impact when hit full on to the object ball (a stun shot) where the two balls are six feet apart, would bring the cue ball back towards you (a screw shot) if the balls were two feet apart.

For the moment, ignore the factors of distance and speed, and ignore too the distinction between stun and screw. Whichever result you want, you must develop the skill of screwing the ball.

Screwing the ball

For a novice, any shot employing screw is far more difficult than the equivalent plain ball shot. It is not unlikely that you have seen it played consistently well only on television. But if you master it, it will give you a huge, probably decisive, advantage over your opponents until you leave your fellow novices far behind.

Why is it difficult? Because it demands everything the plain ball shot does and a lot more besides. As with the plain ball shot you must determine the correct potting angle and succeed with the pot. At the same time, you must determine the correct striking point on the cue ball and the correct strength of shot to achieve the desired amount of backspin. Following through feels less natural than it does on a plain ball shot. You must be able to work backwards from the desired result (the eventual position of the cue ball) to the means of achieving that result. This clearly requires good judgment, based on experience. If, for example, you intended to screw the cue ball back two feet and only screwed it back two inches (an easy error to make), you may be in all sorts of trouble.

Lower the bridge
It should be apparent, but it seems not to be, that the application of screw requires an alteration to the bridge. If you aim to strike the cue ball below centre with the normal bridge you will be striking down on it. That means you will be raising your cue arm, dramatically so if you are attempting maximum screw. Naturally this ruins the horizontal cue action. You come through with a scoop, and

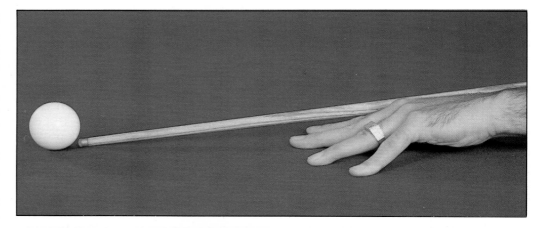

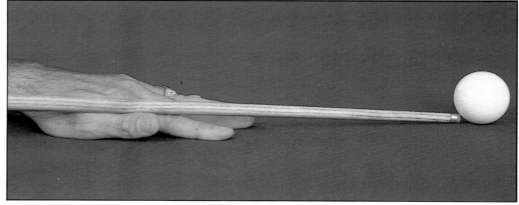

because burying the tip of the cue in the cloth is the snooker player's worst nightmare, you slam on the brakes the instant you hit the ball. So much for follow-through. And so much for backspin, because you cannot get backspin without following through. What you have is a downward stab, not a screw. The chances are that you will miss the pot, unless it is a sitter, and, to add insult to injury, the cue ball will refuse to screw back so much as an inch.

The horizontal cue action and follow-through can only be achieved by lowering the bridge. The extent

In order to keep the cueing action as horizontal as possible when applying screw, the bridge hand should be lowered. The best way to do this is by rolling the bridge hand inwards, as if turning it on its side

to which you lower it is determined by your point of aim on the cue ball. The best way to lower the bridge is to turn the bridge hand inwards, as if you were turning it on to its side. This automatically lowers the thumb and the cue channel. Much of the pressure comes off the little finger, but the bridge should still be solid, with most of the weight on the pad at the base of the thumb. You are now able to strike the cue ball below centre with the horizontal cue action.

With the fear of damaging the cloth removed, it will feel natural to follow through, perhaps not quite so far as with a plain ball shot, but enough to 'feel' the cue ball on the tip of your cue. The slight sensation of 'gripping', as the cue tip bites into the curved surface of the ball, tells you that you have applied screw. It is vital that the cue tip be rounded and well chalked. It is because the professionals use a certain amount of screw in the vast majority of shots that they are in the habit of chalking before every shot.

Players who fail in their attempts with screw usually do so because they strike the cue ball higher than they think they are striking it. They address the ball as though they are going to come through well below centre, but at the last moment they subconsciously raise the line. Fear of an embarrassing miscue, combined with an attempt to use excessive power, is almost invariably the cause. Aim to strike low and *strike* low, which you can do confidently with a horizontal cue. You do not need any extra power to gain screw, although with practice you will find it progressively easier to increase power (when necessary) for greater effect.

Controlled screw

Place a ball on the blue spot with the cue ball about nine inches away, directly in line with a middle pocket. Using normal strength, keep potting the ball using screw. With a little bit of screw the cue ball will stop dead upon impact (a stun shot). With more it will come back (a screw shot), further and further the more screw

Roughly speaking, a screw shot that will bring the cue ball back three feet from a distance of one foot will bring the cue ball back one foot from a distance of three feet

you apply. As your technique improves and your confidence grows, you should be able to screw the cue ball all the way back to the other side pocket. As with potting angles, you must begin to build a memory bank, so that you can associate a particular amount of screw over a certain distance (in this case nine inches) with a predictable result. Good players can screw almost to the inch. When you think you have a pretty fair idea of screwing from nine inches, separate the balls a bit more. And so on. You are now embarked on advanced snooker technique, and it will be apparent to you at once that as your knowledge of screw increases, so the horizons of your game recede. You will soon find that a simple pot with screw is no more difficult than the same simple pot plain ball. On less simple pots, you will find plenty of problems arising from the division of concentration between potting and positions but that is one of the great challenges of the game at any level.

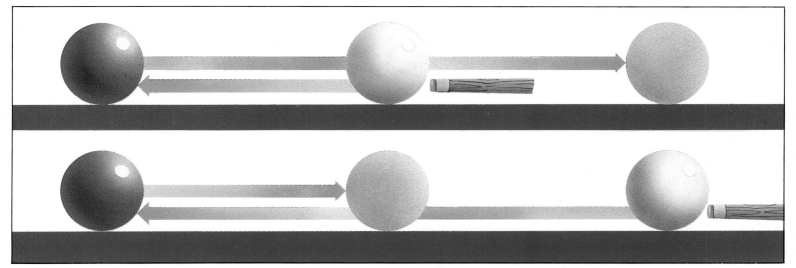

Stun and screw shots

Stun and screw shots, often with the addition of side, form the overwhelming majority in the top-class game. It would be impossible to run up big breaks without them, because they provide the only means of cruising around the black spot for that remorseless red-black, red-black sequence. That is why you hear the words stun and screw continually during a televised match.

Where a screw shot results in the cue ball recoiling upon impact (assuming full ball contact), a stun shot stops it dead in its tracks (again assuming full ball contact). This can be useful, not least because for once you know exactly where the cue ball will be for the next shot. The principle of the stun shot is that the backspin, which is wearing off in the course of the cue ball's journey, must have just enough life left in it at the moment of impact to check the ball's normal forward momentum. The closer the balls are together, the less the backspin required. Too much screw and you have a screw shot, too little and you have stun run-through. Experience must be your guide.

Stun run-through

Stun run-through is a handy variation. Suppose on a straight pot you want to run the cue ball through just a few inches – less than it would run through with a plain ball shot struck normal weight. You could try a very slow plain ball shot, but that is ill-advised because really slow shots expose you to the vagaries of the table (the nap of the cloth, a table that is not perfectly level) or the slightest tremor in your cue arm. Stun run-

Dennis Taylor lines up a screw shot – along with stun, the basis of serious break-building

through is the answer. Strike the cue ball a little higher than you would for that particular stun shot, but still below centre. With normal weight, the cue ball will follow through, but not as far as it would with a plain ball shot.

Full ball shots (stun or screw) provide unambiguous evidence of the application and limitations of screw, because there is no deflection to complicate the equation. A good player should have no difficulty in screwing back eight or ten feet from a distance (cue ball to object ball) of two feet. Assuming you have control, that opens up an enormous range of positional opportunities. At a distance of eight feet, you would need pretty well maximum screw and

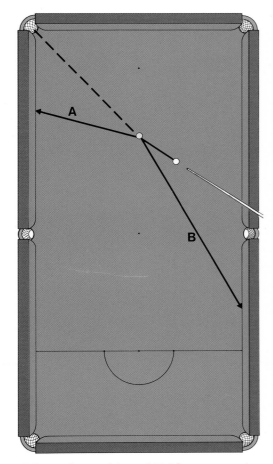

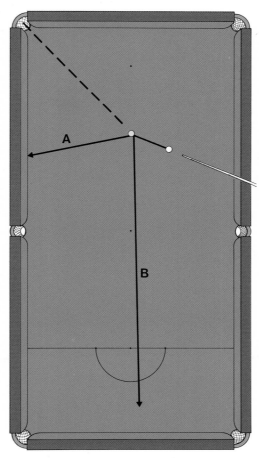

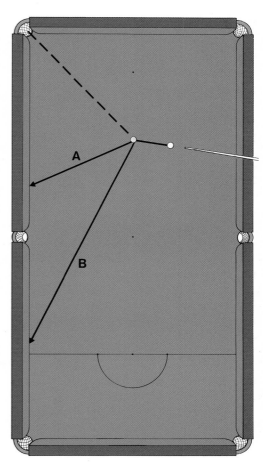

A (run-through) and B (deep screw) are the cue ball's boundaries from a three-quarter ball pink

The half-ball angle gives you less room for cue ball manoeuvre (A to B) than does the three-quarter

The quarter-ball angle further limits the positional range (A to B) available to the cue ball

maximum power to stun the cue ball. You will have seen the professionals screw back half the table from a distance of eight feet, but that is a truly prodigious feat. Combining that much power with perfect timing and accuracy is given only to the Jimmy Whites of this world. If you can screw back a foot or so at six feet and stun at eight, you are doing well.

Useful as screw is for gaining position off a straight pot, it is with angled pots that it really comes into its own. It widens the angle at which the cue ball comes off the object ball. The more screw you apply, the wider the angle. This takes you well and truly off the tramlines. In particular, that congested area around the black spot begins to open up for you. It

may be heavy traffic, but you are no longer careering about out of control. You can go where you want, within the limitations imposed by your mastery of screw. Just as important, you can avoid going where you least want to go, which is in-off. The unavoidable in-off is one of the great hazards of the plain ball shot. Screw makes the unavoidable avoidable.

Using drag

The drag shot has only one application, but it is a common one. When you want to send the cue ball a long way down the table and leave it there, how can you go about it. How can you play a soft shot at a great distance? You could trickle the cue ball the length of the table, but experience will have taught you how dangerous that is. Even if your aim is perfect, the table almost certainly is not, and a really slow shot over a long distance is likely to go critically off line. The answer is drag. If you strike really low with normal strength, imparting plenty of backspin, the cue ball will make most of its journey at speed, only to slow down at the end as the backspin takes its toll. The effect is that of playing a slow shot at much closer range.

Two common situations demand drag. If you have a long pot on a red at the top of the table (say three-quarter ball, with the red a foot or so off the cushion), drag enables you to stay up there for the black. If to play safe you have to send the cue ball from the top of the table deep into baulk, hit the object ball so as to bring it off the baulk cushion and back up the table, meanwhile leaving the cue ball near the baulk cushion, drag is your shot.

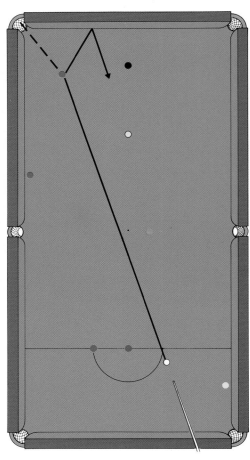

A drag shot here will allow you to pot the red and hold the cue ball for the black

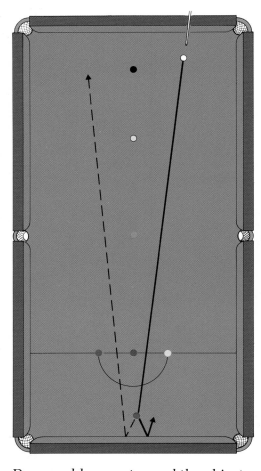

Drag enables you to send the object ball to safety, leaving the cue ball in the baulk area

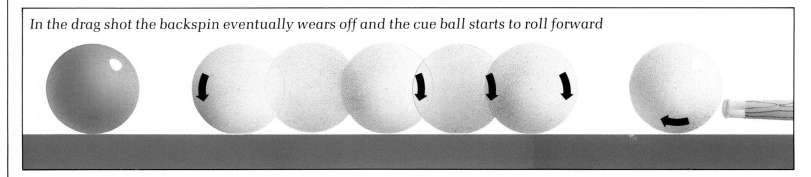

In the drag shot the backspin eventually wears off and the cue ball starts to roll forward

Applying side

Side adds quite fiendish complications to the shot without corresponding benefits – unless and until you understand its workings well and possess good enough technique to employ it properly. The average player frequently misses his pots or messes up his position either because he has inadvertently applied side, or deliberately applied it without a clear understanding of its effects. There should at this stage be no need to labour the point that if you do not know where the cue ball is going to go without side, you are hardly going to be able to gauge the effect of side.

What side does

The principal effect of side is to alter the normal angle at which the cue ball comes off the cushion after contact with the object ball (beforehand if you are using a cushion to try to escape from a snooker). If the cue ball strikes the cushion dead on at a ninety degree angle without side, it will rebound directly back along the line of approach. If it strikes the cushion at that angle with right-hand side it will come off at an angle to the right; with left-hand side to the left. It follows that if it strikes the cushion coming from left to right, right-hand side (called running side) will widen the angle of departure, left-hand side (check side) will narrow it. Coming on to the cushion from right to left, right- and left-hand side will have the opposite effect. Playing the cue ball off the cushions from different angles with right- and left-hand side will quickly show you the extent to which side does this.

Silvino Francisco demonstrates right-hand side. Strike straight through the cue ball, not across it

You apply side by striking the cue ball to the right or left of centre. It is imperative, however, that you strike straight through the cue ball, which means that the line of the shot must be through the point on the cue ball at which you are aiming. You court certain disaster if you get down over a shot as though to play plain ball, decide that you want to use side and simply redirect your cue tip. By striking across the ball you will most certainly swerve it off line – if, that is, you avoid miscueing. The principle is the same as it is over second thoughts about potting angles. You must get up from the shot, adjust your stance slightly in line with your revised intentions, and re-position your bridge so that you are in line with the right or left side of the cue ball.

As with screw, there are two reasons why you might fail to achieve the desired spinning action with side. They are the same two reasons. Either you are not following through or, more likely with side, you are not striking far enough to the side of the cue ball – even though you may think you are. A conscious or subconscious fear of miscueing causes you to drift back to the safety of the centre at the moment of delivering the stroke. That last check on the position of the tip in relation to the cue ball during the final backswing is your invaluable guide.

This matter of actually striking the cue ball where you think you are striking it becomes increasingly critical as you move on to the advanced shots. Consider the combination of deep screw with maximum side. This is an advanced shot in anybody's book, but it is frequently the best or only answer to a tricky positional situation, and it is therefore an essential stroke in any serious player's repertoire. You must strike well below centre, and well to the

Applying side

side – and straight, with follow-through . . . not forgetting to make the pot. You are deliberately accepting very narrow margins for such a shot, and success depends on your striking the cue ball spot on. The better, and therefore more ambitious, a player you become, the more you will realize the difficulty of doing that. Joe Davis was of the opinion that the main reason why he was so good at the game – why he was so much better than you, to put it bluntly – was that he struck the cue ball where he intended to strike it, and you do not. Davis did not mean to be cruelly dismissive by this assertion, merely to focus attention on the fundamental importance of basic technique.

Once you have got the knack of applying it properly, the complexities of side begin in earnest. The purpose of side is to redirect the cue ball late in the lifetime of the shot – after contact with the object ball and a cushion. However, the effects of side operate throughout the shot,

right from the beginning. When you apply right-hand side, the cue ball is initially pushed off course lightly to the *left* by the cue thrust, before the anticlockwise spin brings it back to the *right*. Conversely with left-hand side. The cue ball is therefore describing a slight arc throughout its journey. It may reach the object ball *before* getting back to the true line (if the balls are close together), or *after* crossing over that line (if they are far apart).

A slight change of aim
Obviously there is some particular distance at which the true line is reached at the point of contact, but when using side you will frequently find that you have to alter your normal aim slightly in order to make the pot. This is more a matter of touch than conscious aiming as several factors, such as the condition of the cloth, can have a distinct bearing. And what deviation there is can be minimized by both smooth striking and follow-through.

Speed also affects the equation. The greater the speed, the further the cue ball will travel before the side counteracts the initial thrust in the opposite direction. Say the balls are three feet apart. Played slowly with right-hand side, the cue ball will have recovered from the initial thrust and moved across the line to the right by the time of contact. With normal pace it should be just about on line. Played hard, it will not quite have got there. The nap of the cloth too affects side. The heavier the nap, the greater the effect of spin. It follows from all these variables that long-distance shots played slowly with side are virtually suicidal, since calculating the drift accurately is beyond the capabilities of even the best players. Only by trial and error – and careful observation – will you discover your own safe margins for using side. As a rule you should be chary of going much beyond eighteen inches to the object ball. More than three feet is risky for anyone.

So far, the assumption has been that the shot is played up the table, with the nap. If it is played towards baulk, against the nap, it becomes even trickier. This is because running against the nap the spin works in reverse. With right-hand side, there is the usual initial thrust to the left. But instead of the right-hand side then bringing the ball back to the right, it continues to push it out to the left throughout its journey. This makes the slow shot with side utterly treacherous, and the best players discount it out of hand. Yet it is not uncommon to see club players attempting to hit a slow shot the

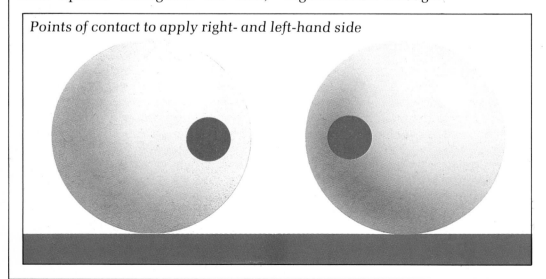

Points of contact to apply right- and left-hand side

length of the table, against the nap, with maximum side. They should consider themselves fortunate if they even make contact with the object ball.

Assuming you can apply side correctly, and are prepared to do so within sensible limitations of distance and speed, there remains yet another complication. Side slightly alters the angle at which the object ball is thrown by the cue ball. You must adjust the potting angle accordingly. Take, for example, a half-ball pot up table on a spotted black, with the cue ball to the right of the black. If you strike the black at the half-ball angle for a plain ball shot with right-hand side, the black will go to the left of the pocket – too fine. With left-hand side it will miss to the right – too thick. At this point you could be forgiven for thinking that side is more trouble than it is worth, but in fact experienced players use side so much that they quite automatically make the necessary adjustments to the potting angles.

The myth of transmitted side

Apart from altering slightly the angle at which it is thrown, side has no discernible effect on the object ball. There is not a shred of evidence to support the widely-held belief that side is transmitted to the object ball. However, while ignoring the myth of transmitted side, it is worth considering the one particular circumstance that its believers always bring up in evidence. That is where you are potting down the cushion.

This is always a difficult shot because you have the minimum of

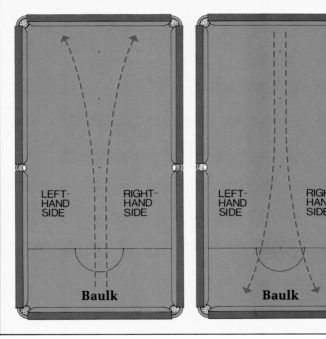

Baulk end

Direction of nap ▶

The nap of the cloth runs up the table from baulk. You must understand the effect of the nap when using side. When playing away from baulk, right-hand side takes the ball to the right, left-hand side to the left. When playing towards baulk, right-hand side will take the ball to the left, left-hand side to the right

pocket to aim for. According to the myth of transmitted side, running side (right-hand side if you are approaching from left to right) increases the chances of making the pot. The theory is that the anticlockwise spin on the cue ball is transmitted to the object ball, which is therefore inclined to hug the cushion as it runs along towards the pocket. The truth is that most players do indeed find it easier to make the pot with running side, but transmitted side is not the correct explanation. The way to make the pot, with or without side, is to strike the cushion ever-so fractionally before the object ball, with quite a soft shot. Running side may have two

beneficial effects in this instance. First, as the cue ball approaches the cushion and object ball, which it must hit almost simultaneously, it will be curving slightly inwards, so that at the point of impact it is marginally more behind the object ball, in line with the pot. Second, running side widens the angle at which the cue ball comes off the cushion as it strikes the object ball. This effectively keeps the cue ball on the potting line fractionally longer than would otherwise be the case. The combined effect of these two factors should not be exaggerated, but if running side increases your confidence with this shot by all means use it.

The swerve shot

Swerve is an extreme form of side. With side, the cue ball curves to a degree, which generally speaking is a nuisance because it adds an unwanted variable to the shot. Sometimes, however, the curving effect can be turned to advantage. If you are in a position where you can almost but not quite achieve a potting angle, because of an intervening ball, side may do the trick. In the same way, side may be sufficient to get you out of the mildest of snookers. But if you are well and truly blocked by an intervening ball, ordinary side will not get you out of the trouble. A great many snookers demand an escape route off one or more cushions, but by no means all. Swerve can be the answer.

To play a swerve shot you break the rule of horizontal cueing. You strike downward on the cue ball, with side. This exaggerates the initial thrust off line before the side takes effect, thereby curving the cue ball right around the intervening ball to get to the object ball. It is not enough merely to raise the butt in order to get the downward angle (something like forty five degrees, although this will vary depending upon the desired swerve). The bridge should be raised as well, with the palm coming right off the table. Avoid the common error of striking high on the cue ball. Strike it below centre to maximize the swerve. And break the rule about following through. There should be almost no follow-through with a swerve shot.

This shot requires considerable practice, in order to discover the combination of downward angle,

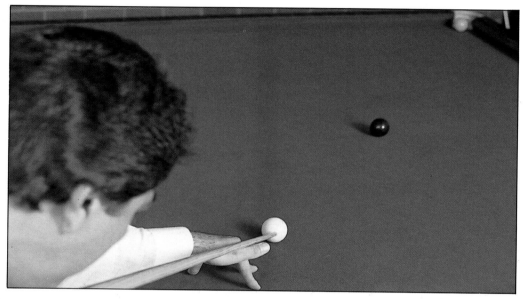

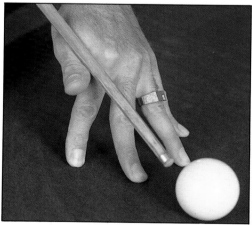

amount of side and strength of shot to achieve any particular line of swerve. Except by accident, it is quite impossible to be absolutely accurate with swerve, and it must therefore be viewed as a purely defensive stroke. You might indeed pot a ball sitting over the pocket with a swerve shot, but then you could pot a real sitter using the wrong end of the cue.

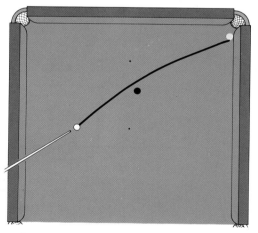

Silvino Francisco demonstrates the swerve shot, bending the cue ball around the black in order to pot the pink. Swerve is an extreme form of side, involving a downward strike on the cue ball

The massé shot

What swerve is to side, massé is to swerve. It is swerve to the ultimate degree. The massé shot plays a far greater role in billiards than it does in snooker, but to be a complete snooker player you must learn it. The massé is called for when a swerve shot would not get the cue ball back from its outward curve in time to make contact with the object ball. This arises where there is only a short distance between cue ball and intervening ball, or between intervening ball and object ball, or both.

The exotic sounding massé shot looks extraordinary because it is at complete variance with every other shot in the game. The cue is struck downwards, practically from the vertical. The cue grip is normal, but a little shorter than usual. The elbow of the bridge arm is wedged against the side of the body for steadiness. The shoulders are as braced as they can be. The bridge hand is completely transformed. Three fingers form a

tripod, while the thumb and index finger (the knuckle, really) form a channel of sorts. The wrist is sharply arched, and the palm is facing outwards. It is altogether a weird-looking stroke, but a highly effective one.

Not surprisingly, it requires a great deal of practice to work out the various degrees of spin required to bend the ball to your will. How the cue ball will spin depends upon where you hit it – obviously either right or left, as required, but there is more to it than that. If you come down on the front of the upper surface you will get topspin. The ball will initially go slowly backwards, and then leap forwards with a strong combination of topspin and side. If you come down on the back of the ball you will get backspin. The ball will

The massé shot, played by Silvino Francisco. It is an extreme form of swerve, involving an almost vertical strike

initially go slowly forwards, and then race backwards with extreme side. As with swerve, there should be no follow-through (which in this case would bury the cue tip in the cloth).

The power shot

The true power shot, as opposed to a shot played with considerable pace, is immensely difficult, and most professionals use it sparingly. The problem with it is that it forces you to break the cardinal rules concerning cue action. The longer backswing needed to generate real power, the hard strike and full follow-through conspire to play havoc with that smooth, sweetly-grooved action.

There is almost bound to be movement of the shoulder as you feel yourself putting your whole body into the shot, and the head will inevitably rise. You must do what you can to minimize such movement – by bracing yourself even more firmly than usual, making an especially firm bridge and so on – but movement and therefore less accuracy is the price you pay for a power shot. Follow the

example of the professionals, and only attempt a power shot when you have no other means of gaining position. Having said that, observe how a player like Jimmy White, who plays power shots superbly, obtains his power not with a massive swing but by maximum controlled acceleration through the cue ball. Uncontrolled power spells disaster, so resist the temptation to have a bash.

Awkward bridging

Snooker would be a much easier game if it were always possible to form a bridge in the orthodox manner. That it is not so is a problem that confronts the novice right from the start. He finds that his previous shot, or his opponent's, has left the cue ball too near a cushion for the bridge to be formed comfortably – if at all. Or he faces the even more intimidating task of cueing over one or more intervening balls. Really awkward bridging is hazardous for even the best players, and they must cope with it continually because leaving the cue ball close to, and preferably tight against, a cushion is the central feature of most safety play. For the novice, and even the player of reasonable skill, awkward bridging can trigger panic. There is a temptation to hurry the shot – to get the unpleasant experience over with – and this almost certainly is to transform a difficulty into a disaster. The vital rule, therefore, is to approach the situation calmly and deliberately.

Steve Davis (top) is cueing close to the cushion. Note the raised bridge, supported only by the fingers and the heel of the hand. Davis again (right) is attempting to escape from a snooker. This time he is able to form a near-normal bridge, with the forearm in support

With only his finger pads on the table (above), Davis has just played the cue ball away from the cushion. This is the bridge that allows you to play a power shot with the cue ball tucked in under the cushion. It is extremely difficult to keep the bridge hand rigid when it is up in the air and there is only finger contact with the table. This is no shot for novices. The closer the cue ball is to the cushion the more difficult the cueing becomes, because you have less of the cue ball to see and therefore the higher up you must strike it

Awkward bridging

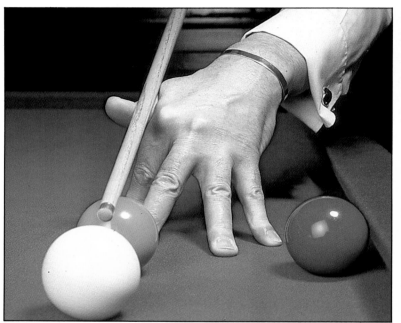 

Front and side views (above) of the bridge generally regarded as the most difficult of all – the one that allows you to reach the cue ball over an intervening ball. Apart from the fact that it is up in the air, it is much like the conventional bridge, the fingers well spread and the thumb and forefinger forming a deep channel for the cue. Keep as much of your finger pads on the table as possible – they are your sole contact with it. Miscueing is always a danger because you are striking high up on the cue ball with a downward thrust

The loop bridge (left) is favoured by some players for delicate close-in work, because they feel it minimizes cue wobble. Some also like to use it for deep screw shots because it enables deeper striking

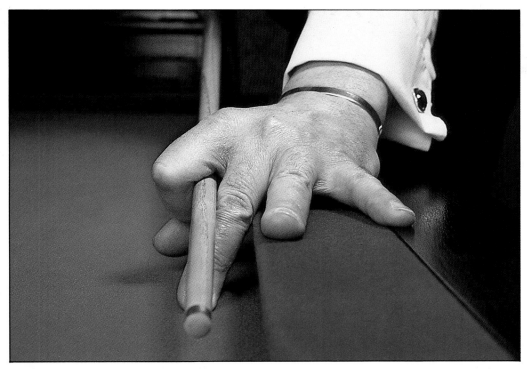

The loop bridge, rarely used when the conventional bridge can be comfortably formed, comes into its own when you have to play a shot down the cushion. The bridge is formed by looping the forefinger over the cue and resting it against the thumb. Guard against tightening the grip on the cue, which must run freely. Dennis Taylor and Kirk Stevens (left and right) demonstrate the loop bridge as it is formed along either side cushion

Using the various rests

No player welcomes a position from which he must use the rest or, worse, the spider or one of the longer cues and rests (the half butt and the three-quarter butt). Any of these implements necessarily restricts cue control. There is a temptation, therefore, to go almost to any lengths to avoid using them. You will have seen ordinary players (*not* the pros) both overreaching and accepting a ludicrously large distance between bridge and cue ball. It is also common enough for players to shun the rest and thereby ignore perfectly reasonable potting opportunities. Either of these mistaken practices will hinder your progress. The rest and its fellows must be viewed in the same light as the various supplementary bridges. They are there to help you when you need them. Learn to use them correctly.

Steve Davis prepares for a shot using the rest. Note how the left forearm is firmly bolted to the table, the right shoulder forward and the body to the right of the cue. The eyes are below the line of the shot, which is a straight push from the hand, the power generating from the forearm only. The rest itself (inset) has both a horizontal aspect (shown) and a vertical one, the choice being determined by where you want to strike the cue ball

The spider and longer rests are there to get you out of situations that would otherwise be impossible. Tony Knowles bridges over the pack with a variation of the spider called the 'swan neck' (top left).
Neal Foulds uses the normal spider and cue extension (top), while yet another version of the spider is available for truly fiendish positions (above). The three-quarter butt allows Silvino Francisco to reach the black (left)

Cue control and cue ball control are means to an end – the end being to play good snooker, winning snooker. As your skills improve, and your confidence grows, you will automatically find yourself devoting attention to the tactics of the game. It is the tactics, after all, that make snooker so absorbing to watch and so challenging to play. In the end, tactical snooker is about choosing the best shot to suit the circumstances. The complexities of snooker are such that shot selection is not obvious, much of the time. Is it worth taking on a difficult pot in order to initiate a possible break? Or would a killing safety shot be likely to reap greater rewards? To know the answer is to give yourself the best chance of exploiting your skills, and thwarting your opponent's.

Break-building

Because snooker is a game of immeasurable variety the subject of break-building is inexhaustible. No player has ever got to the end of it and none ever will. If you were to suggest to Steve Davis that it must all be pretty old hat to him by now he would realize you knew nothing about snooker. He will remain fascinated by break-building for the rest of his playing life. It is the core of his (and any) game, and in his quest for snooker perfection he will ponder it, practise it and dismay his opponents with deadly demonstrations of it for as long as he remains on top of the world of snooker. His safety play is of course exemplary, but it is his superior break-building, over the long haul of a long season, that first put him and still keeps him at the front of the pack.

You should consider it reassuring that the most exhilarating aspect of snooker is also the most important. At whatever level you play, that will always be the case. The rank novice who pays attention to his cue action and studies the angles will quickly gain a measure of confidence in potting. He will quickly get into the habit of thinking in positional terms, which means he will stand an excellent chance of following a red with a colour. For the novice, that two-ball sequence is in itself a useful break, and he may well extend it with another red and colour. He will beat the spots off a fellow novice who contents himself with potting the easiest red in the hope that a colour will then miraculously present itself. The club player who really applies himself to the challenge of scoring twenty four points when he is amongst three loose reds around the black spot will always pull away from an opponent who is pleased to take a red and a black and then run for safety. And so it goes, right to the top of the game.

Control around the black
Nothing could be more apparent from watching televised snooker than the supreme importance of control around the black. The really enormous breaks feature it almost exclusively, even if in the course of some total or near total clearances the player is forced to take the odd lower-value colour in order to sustain the break. Useful, and even frame-winning breaks can be and are fashioned around the pink, but such breaks appear to be constructed rather painfully. Certainly break-building on the pink never rattles along with the apparent ease that you are accustomed to seeing when the action is around the black.

An obvious reason why players favour the black is that it is the highest scoring ball on the table. But that is not the principal reason. By design or happy accident, the game was devised in such a way that the most valuable colour happens to be far and away the best positioned for break-building. As play normally unfolds, no other colour is so well placed for establishing and continuing the red-colour, red-colour sequence. The pink on its spot will go into any pocket (assuming a favourable lie of the balls), but it is much further from the top pockets than the black is. More to the point, it is much further from the top cushion. It is the fact that the black spot is close to the reds, close to the top pockets and close to the top cushion that sets it apart as the premier ball for break-building. Endless use of the top cushion is made in the black ball game. It is quite inconceivable to imagine a really big break made without it. It is fair to say that if the rules of snooker were changed by swopping black and blue spots, say, players would stay at the top of the table and content themselves with the lower-value colour. As for the baulk colours, they play no part in serious break-building except as a fall-back position for keeping a break going when it would otherwise be stymied.

Willie Thorne (left) is regarded
by his fellow professionals
as a tremendous break-builder.
John Parrott (below) is typical
of the younger stars who
demonstrate a natural flair for
amassing big breaks

The red-black sequence

You will encounter endless permutations of break-building opportunities around the black spot, and practice will help you to gain assurance when presented with them. There are two golden rules to keep in mind (apart from making the pots). First, be careful about leaving yourself straight on the black. If you do, you restrict your positional range to the line of the shot (forward, backward or stone dead), doubly disadvantageous because it rules out possible use of the top cushion. There are occasions when a six-inch screw back or six-inch run-through are all you need, but often dead straight will get you into positional trouble where a wide range of other angles will not. Second, clear the path between the black spot and both top pockets at the earliest opportunity. That way you maximize your scope for potting the black, which is particularly important if you come a little adrift in positional terms after potting a red.

To practise, you can simply scatter a few reds in the vicinity of the black and take it from there. If you group four reds as indicated, all the principal features of black-ball play will present themselves.

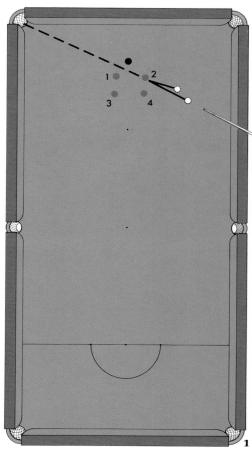

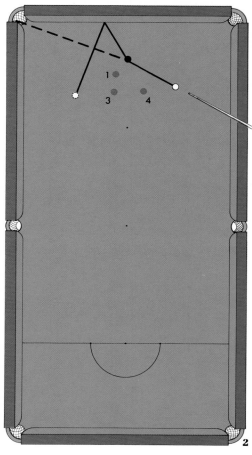

1 Taking Red 2 straight into the top left pocket is an arbitrary choice. Screw back to leave a three-quarter ball angle on the black.

2 Pot the black plain ball and bounce off the cushion to leave a choice of all the other reds. If instead of doing that you were to stun off the top cushion, thereby coming back the other side of the reds, you would be committing yourself to Red 3. In general, do not attempt to gain pinpoint position on one red when you can have adequate position on several.

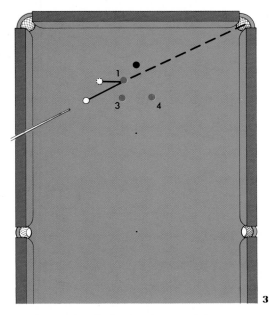

3

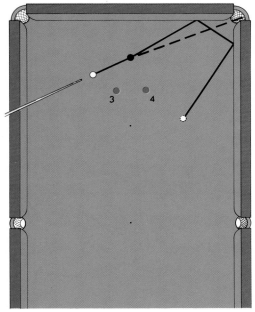

4

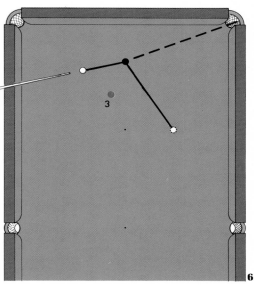

6

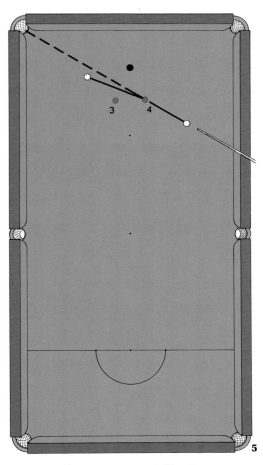

5

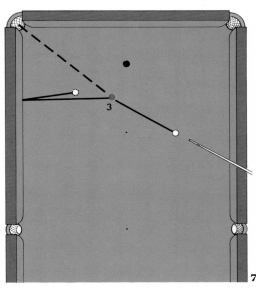

7

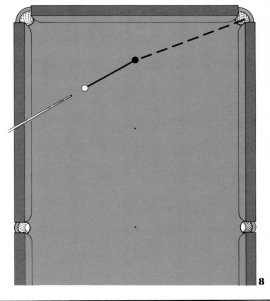

8

3 You are just off straight on Red 1, which is ideal because by getting rid of Red 1 both remaining reds become pottable in either pocket. A little screw shot should leave you with that familiar three-quarter ball angle on the black.

4 In fact, you have come slightly too straight on the black (but not dead straight, which would rule out the top cushion). Pot the black with top and right-hand side, to bring the cue ball off top and side cushions into position for both remaining reds. When

using side, it is especially important to follow through smoothly because you are not striking the cue ball at its point of maximum density (ie, the middle).

5 You are straight on Red 4, so simply run through for the black, aiming again for the three-quarter ball angle.

6 Screw off the black for the final red.

7 Pot the red plain ball and bounce off the cushion to leave yourself comfortably on the black.

8 Pot black.

Sustaining a break by using the blue

You will often find yourself in a position where the only pottable (or easily pottable) red must result in your sending the cue ball down the table away from the black and pink. Sometimes you will have to go all the way down to the baulk colours; other times you will be able to pull up for the blue. In this example, you are too thin on the red to hold the cue ball for the pink. Even pocket weight on

Having come baulk side of blue in potting the previous red, Steve Davis is now perfectly placed to come back to the top of the table

the red (dangerous at this distance) would only succeed in putting the cue ball somewhere near the blue but the wrong (ie, baulk) side of it and as thin as quarter-ball on the pink. You should accept that you are at least for the moment out of business on the pink.

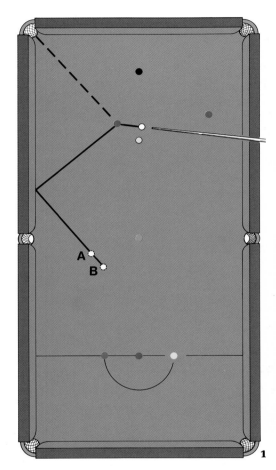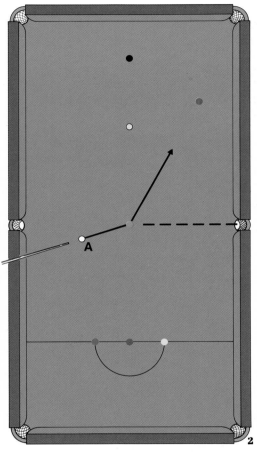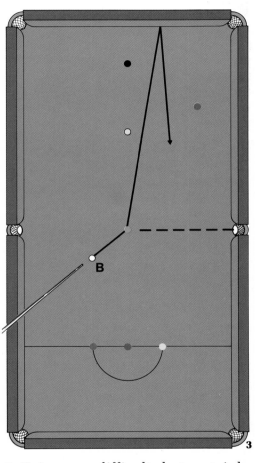

1 Go positively for a positional shot on the blue, rather than just hope it emerges. Pot the red with screw and a touch of left-hand side. Ideally you want to be three-quarter ball on the blue (A), but half-ball will do (B).

2 If A, simply stun the blue and you will come nicely on to the last red, with black to follow.

3 B is more difficult, but certainly achievable. Stun the cue ball off the top cushion with a touch of left-hand side. In either case, once you are firmly on that final red the table is at your mercy.

Sometimes a player slightly over-hits and comes past both A and B, but then is able to rescue himself by potting the blue straight to the corner pocket. Take this as a favourable run of the balls and do not rely on it.

Sustaining a break by using the baulk colours

When you run out of position on the black and pink, the blue is not always available to rescue you. It may be near a cushion, or some reds may be blocking its path to a suitable pocket. Alternatively, the blue itself may be in the open but you have left yourself on a red in such a way that in potting it you will not be able to hold the cue ball for the blue into a middle pocket. You are therefore forced to look to the baulk colours to sustain your break. In such circumstances, go positively for position on one or more of the baulk colours, rather than simply float the cue ball towards baulk in the hope that something suitable will materialize.

Steve Davis lines up to the yellow, confident of potting it and bringing the cue ball back up the table to achieve position on one of the remaining reds

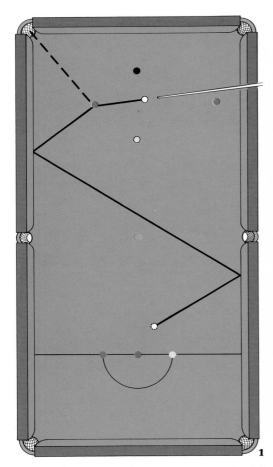

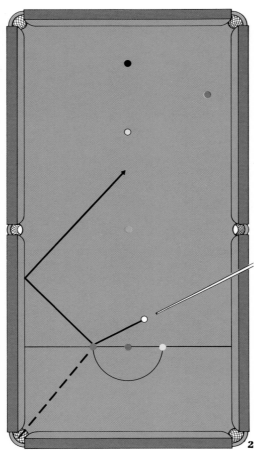

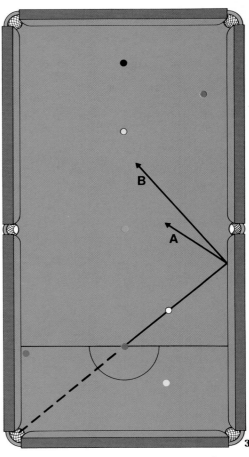

1 In this example, you cannot hold for the blue because the potting angle on the red is too thin. Take the cue ball off both side cushions for a baulk colour. Any one of the three will do, which gives you a good margin. The only rule is never to go beyond the baulk line when trying to sustain a break using a baulk colour. From behind the baulk line you could easily lay a snooker on the remaining red, but that is distinctly inferior to keeping the break going – in this case right through to a clearance, which is decidedly on.

2 You are on all three colours, but the three-quarter ball green is ideal for screwing back up for the final red.

3 In this example you are straight on the brown, with the yellow and green well away from their spots. A simple screw shot would take you along path A, but if you play the shot with screw and left-hand side the cue ball will follow path B. In either case you should pot the last red, but by taking the 'B' option you will be able to make the red so much easier that you can devote more of your concentration to leaving the most advantageous angle on the black to gain position on the yellow.

Clearing the colours

Even in the most closely fought matches, the top professionals routinely defeat each other by thumping margins in individual frames. That is because they are all capable of taking decisive advantage of positional openings when they occur. Frequently a good opening appears very early in the frame – even from the break-off – which means that the frame may be effectively decided then and there. You will often have seen one player sitting quietly in his chair while his opponent runs up an opening break of eighty or more. From that point he is just a spectator like everyone else, curious to see how far the break will be extended. He has lost the frame, painlessly enough in this case since once that big break began to unfold the outcome was beyond his control. There is every chance that he will turn the tables next frame, and get away with as big a break or bigger.

When it's all on the colours

At less exalted levels of play, frame scores, as opposed to match scores, tend to be nothing like so lopsided. Where a good break is considered to be twenty, there is ample opportunity to keep alive in a frame. For players of roughly equal ability, it is the rule rather than the exception for them to arrive at the colours with everything still to play for. That being so, nothing could be more useful than knowing how to go about clearing the colours in a single trip to the table. This is not as easy as it is so often made to look on television, but if you understand the basic principles involved you will at least be able to make a realistic

attempt. How you fare thereafter will depend upon your ability to execute positional strokes as you intend them.

Obviously the six colours can be left anywhere on the table, some or even all of them in unpottable positions, the cue ball miles from the yellow or whatever. However, the better the standard of play, the more likely they are to be sitting on their spots. For practice, assume that they are, that you have potted the final red, followed it with a colour and deliberately come into ideal position on the yellow. It is very important that you get into the habit of approaching the final red-colour sequence with yellow in mind.

Make the pots easy

Note how comparatively simple all the pots are, given accurate positional strokes. Consider how easily the sequence can break down with one bad positional shot. You may rescue yourself temporarily with a good pot, but the chances are you will have to follow it with an even better pot. How long will you be able to sustain a break that makes such heavy demands on your potting ability?

You may be interested to know that Steve Davis attempts this routine literally endlessly. That is, he clears from yellow to black, and in potting the black brings the cue ball back down the table for position on the yellow. Then he re-spots the balls and starts all over again. And so on, and on . . .

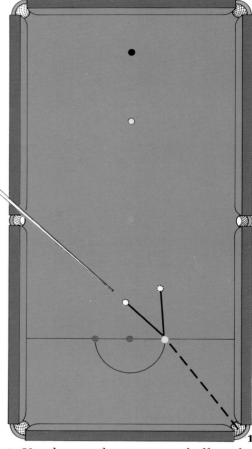

1 You have a three-quarter ball angle – possibly slightly fuller – on the yellow. Screw back for the green. Should you be somewhere between three-quarter and half-ball on the yellow you would have to stun the cue ball off the side cushion to come on to the same position for the green.

2 Three-quarter ball on the green is ideal, although anything between that and straight will do nicely. Less than three-quarter and you will need to come off the side cushion for the brown. If you go more than a fraction

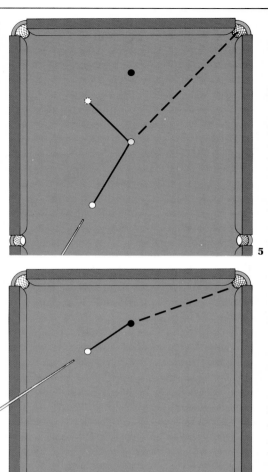

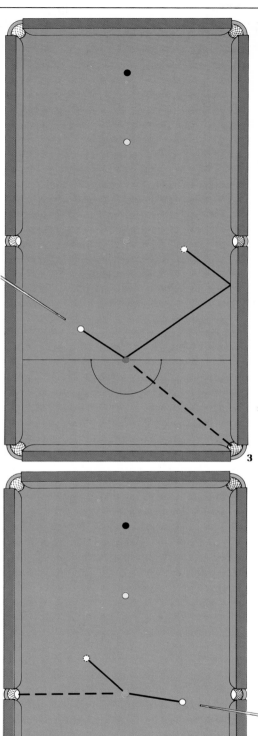

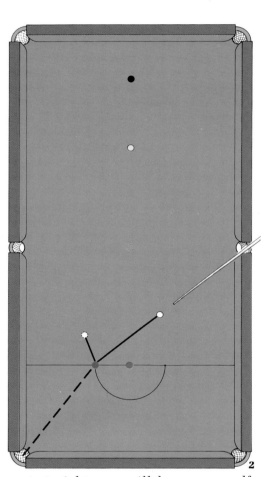

past straight you will leave yourself the more difficult task of potting the green and bouncing off the bottom cushion for position on the brown. Pot the green and screw back for the brown, aiming to leave yourself between half-ball and three-quarter ball on it.

3 You are nearly half-ball on the brown, which is fine. This is the most testing positional shot of the sequence because of the distance the cue ball must travel. Pot the brown and stun off the side cushion to come

three-quarter ball on the blue. If you come much less than three-quarter ball you will have difficulty in holding the cue ball for the pink. Straight on the blue will leave you with an eminently missable pink. But the worst thing you can do is to get above the blue. You would then be sending

the cue ball away from the pink as you potted the blue. You see the professionals negotiate this difficulty with ease, bringing the cue ball around off three cushions for the pink, but not only do they have the cue power for the job, they have a fine, fast-moving championship cloth to help them.

4 Pot the three-quarter ball blue and run through for a three-quarter ball pink. Again, the real pitfall here is to run past straight on the pink. There is no problem if you can still pot the pink three-quarter ball and come off the side cushion, but if you leave a half-ball pot you will have an un-favourable angle to get on the black.

5 Pot the three-quarter ball pink and stun for black.

6 A simple three-quarter ball black.

Clearing the colours from the 'D'

There can be any number of variations in the early stages of clearing all the colours from their spots, depending upon the position on the yellow. The positional shot from black to yellow is obviously one of the most critical in the game. Your intention will be to gain ideal position, but you will not always succeed. Sometimes this will be because you simply play a poor or mediocre shot in potting the black. Other times, you will have left yourself on the black in such a way that in potting it you have no realistic chance of getting down the table for yellow. With a reasonable angle a long or longish pot on the yellow is quite feasible, although at a critical stage in a frame it carries considerable risk. Finally, you may find yourself with less than ideal position on the yellow through no fault of your own. Your opponent has gone in-off, leaving the colours on their spots. You are therefore starting the clearance with the cue ball in the 'D'. Because this particular circumstance crops up now and again in real play, clearing the colours from the 'D' is worth practising.

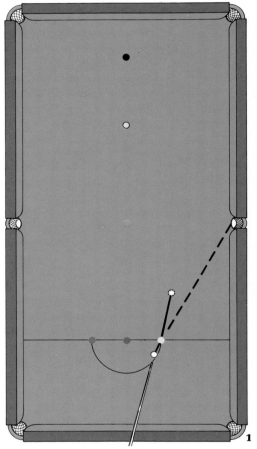
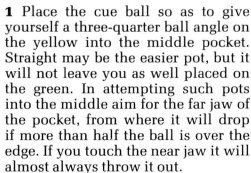

1

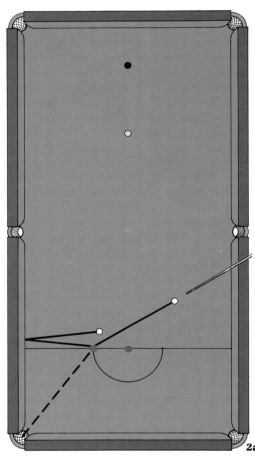

2a

1 Place the cue ball so as to give yourself a three-quarter ball angle on the yellow into the middle pocket. Straight may be the easier pot, but it will not leave you as well placed on the green. In attempting such pots into the middle aim for the far jaw of the pocket, from where it will drop if more than half the ball is over the edge. If you touch the near jaw it will almost always throw it out.

2a The pot on the yellow, assuming you make it, should leave you more or less half-ball on the green — three-quarter ball if you can get the cue ball to travel further. The pot is not difficult, but you have a bewildering array of positional opportunities on the brown. You can play the green slowly and bring the cue ball off the side cushion to achieve conventional position on the brown (as in the earlier sequence). The difficulty with attempting this shot is that you must play it slowly, and slow shots, especially against or across the nap, have a habit of drifting off line. On a poor table you can almost guarantee it.

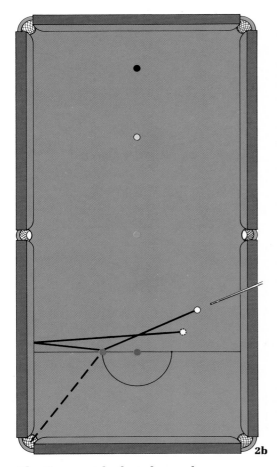

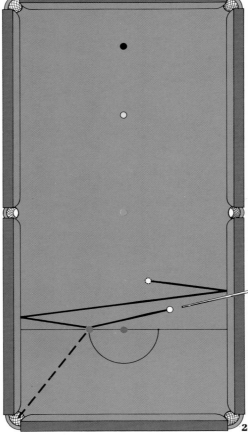

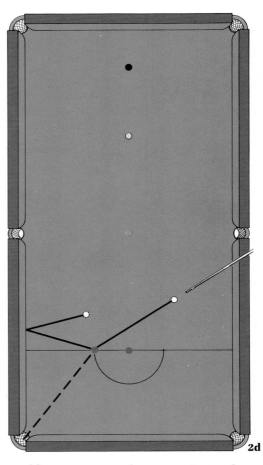

2b

2c

2d

2b To avoid that hazard you can play the shot with greater strength, attempting to bring the cue ball back to the other side of the brown, so that the brown can be potted in the same baulk pocket as the green.

2c Or you can play it stronger still, to come off both side cushions and leave the cue ball a little further up table but still on the brown.

2d Either 2b or 2c is feasible, but this is better. If you stun the green with medium pace you should obtain good

position off one cushion. Note that you need to be able to play all these shots, not necessarily in clearing the colours, but because all of them may be demanded at some stage of the frame.

From there, you continue the clearance as previously described. Whatever the position from which you begin to clear the spotted colours, you must aim to sort yourself out by the time you get to the brown, because the positional shot from brown to blue is a critical one. Yellow, green

and brown are in close proximity, but for blue you are moving into a different area of the table. It is admittedly possible to make a pot on the blue from virtually anywhere on the table and achieve position on the pink, but you would not want to gamble a frame on it. Even for the professionals, brown for blue is likely to be the key shot in the colour clearance.

Clearing the colours (the hard way)

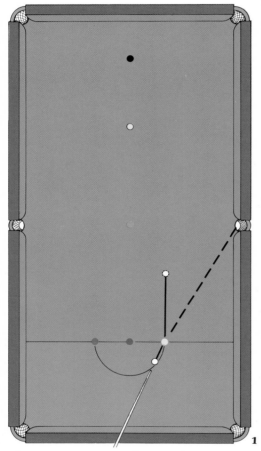

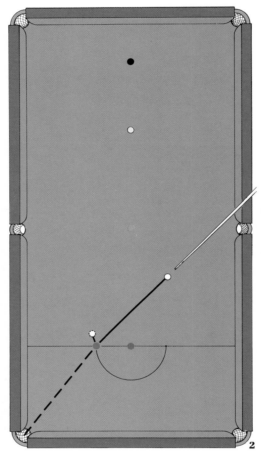

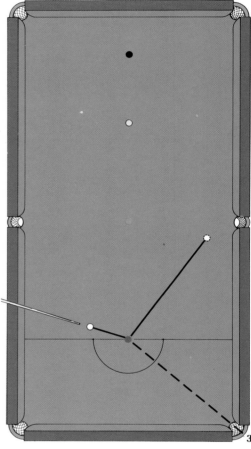

This is a very advanced exercise, indeed a testing one even for the professionals. It provides a harsh examination of anyone's cue ball control.

1 Pot the yellow three-quarter ball into the middle pocket, running through to come almost straight on the green.

2 Screw from the green to three-quarter ball on the brown.

3 Screw sharply from the brown to leave a three-quarter ball or slightly fuller angle on the blue. There is not much margin of error here, and accuracy is difficult, to say the least.

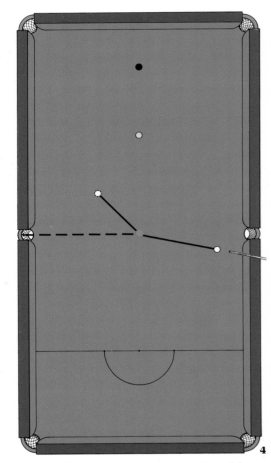

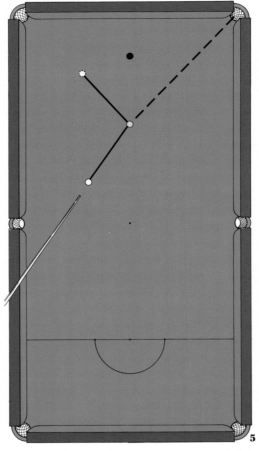

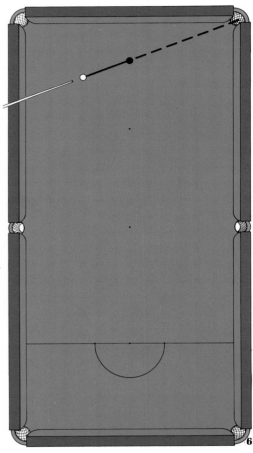

4 A plain ball shot on the blue, pocket weight, coming three-quarter ball on to the pink.

5 Stun the pink, to come as straight as possible on to the black.

6 Stun the black.

If you can do all that, you may with some justification consider that you can afford to give this book to a less accomplished friend.

The line-up

This is a first-rate practice routine, much favoured by professionals. You do not have to be of their standard to profit from it, but you must have progressed to a point where positional play is within your grasp. You must, in other words, have an adequate command of screw and stun strokes, and that implies a reasonable understanding of where the cue ball is likely to wind up after you have played them.

The fifteen reds are arranged as shown in diagram 1, with all the colours on their spots. For the opening shot you can place the cue ball where you wish. Pot a red, then any colour, then another red, another colour and so on. See how far you get without breaking down. Note your score and keep trying to improve on it. When you get to the stage at which you can clear the fifteen reds you will be a good player indeed. Along the way, you will learn a vast amount about positional play, and what you learn will be directly applicable to countless break-building opportunities in the future.

The sequence can be played in an infinite number of ways, and as long as you can keep potting the balls, one is as good as another. The example analysed here is as it was actually played by Clive Everton. It will pay you to study it closely, and more than once. In terms of break-building, and the sort of thinking as well as stroke-play that has to go into it, it is a complete lesson.

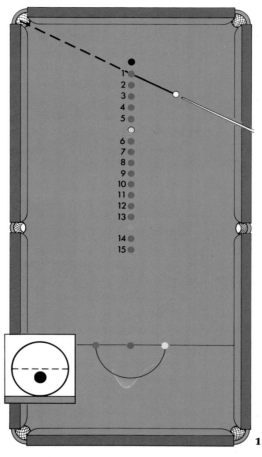

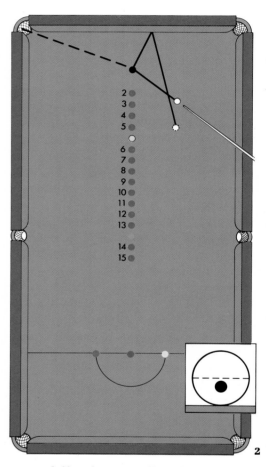

1 Choose what red you want, but Red 1 is as good as any. Straight pot into the top pocket, screwing back for position on the black. The screw must be carefully controlled, as always. Uncontrolled screw is worse than useless. Not far enough and you will be right on top of the black with a quarter-ball angle on it. That pot can be difficult, and the cue ball awkward to control. Screw back too far and you will come almost straight on the black. You will have increased the distance between cue ball and object ball, thereby making the next pot more difficult — really difficult if you have come close enough to the cushion to necessitate awkward bridging. And you will have too thick an angle on the black to gain position easily on another red. The ideal is about three-quarter ball, as here.

2 Pot the black and stun off the top cushion, aiming to come back into position for Red 2 and Red 3. The worst pitfall here is to leave yourself short — above Red 2. It would not matter if you played a little over strength, coming on to Red 4. Further than that

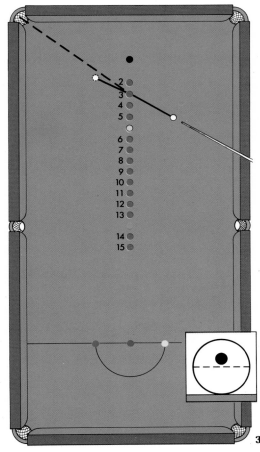

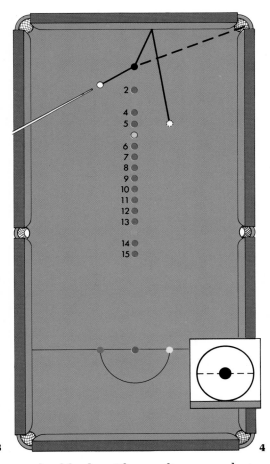

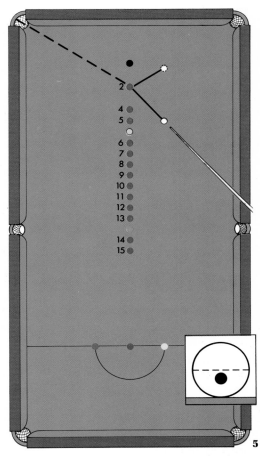

brings you towards the side cushion. Too much screw will widen the angle at which the cue ball comes on to the top cushion, in which case it will end up close to the side cushion. There is a general point here. Always try to leave yourself far enough off the cushions so that you can make your bridge reasonably comfortably on the bed of the table.

3 You have many choices for the next red, but consider Red 2 and Red 3. For Red 2 the potting angle is just too thin to allow you to hold position

on the black with a soft screw shot. You would have to stun off the top cushion to get on to the black. That would not be particularly difficult, but it is not advisable to bring a cushion into play when you have an equally good shot that does not require it. When you use a cushion, you have two factors to take into account: the speed of the table and the speed of the cushions. It is easier to deal with the speed of the table alone. Red 3 is just as good a shot, so it is the better choice. It is three-quarter ball or a little fuller, so run through, aiming to

leave yourself with something like a half-ball angle on the black. At this stage, Red 3 is better than Red 2 for strategic reasons as well. It opens a gap between remaining reds. As the break continues, such gaps become important because they increase the positional margins of error.

4 Pot the black plain ball at slow-medium pace. Pace is everything with plain ball shots, because it is your only control. The object here is for the cue ball to come off the top cushion into position on Red 2. That

The line-up

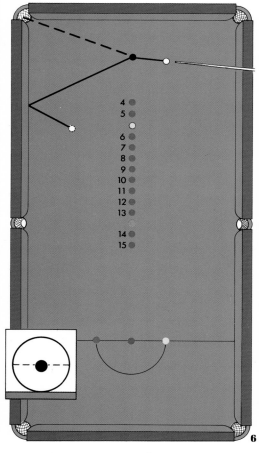

means you want to be roughly level with Red 4 and Red 5, to leave yourself a three-quarter ball angle on Red 2. Falling badly short would be serious. Coming too far would not be as serious because there is always Red 4, and several possibilities for the middle pocket.

5 This three-quarter ball angle on Red 2 is perfect. It allows you to screw gently back for the black. The important thing here is not to finish dead straight on the black. If you do, you will then have to screw straight back

off the side cushion for the following shot. By no means impossible, but the trick always is to make minimal demands on your technique. Worse than dead straight on the black would be to wind up above it. Try *never* to leave yourself above the black. Cut-back shots are always more difficult because the pocket is out of vision. In this particular case, depending upon the angle, a cut-back shot would send the cue ball somewhere into the reds. If you start to scatter the reds around, anything could happen.

6 Three-quarter ball on the black is fine. Play it plain ball, aiming to bring the cue ball a foot or so off the side cushion. This will leave you several choices. You could, if you chose, screw the cue ball directly up beside the reds, thereby avoiding the use of the cushion, but it would be slightly more difficult, with no prospect of positional benefit.

7 Now is the time to turn your back on the red-black sequence, and open up some space between the blue and pink spots. Otherwise, you will find

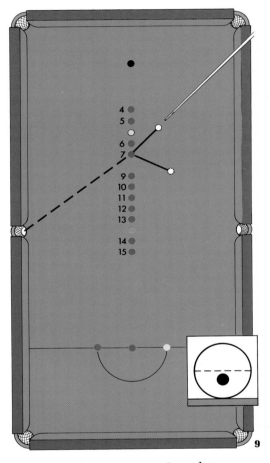

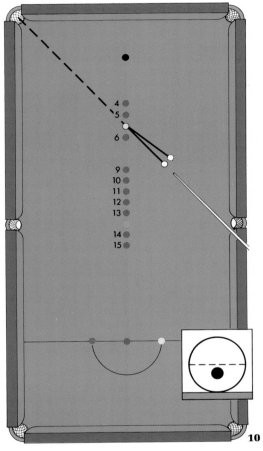

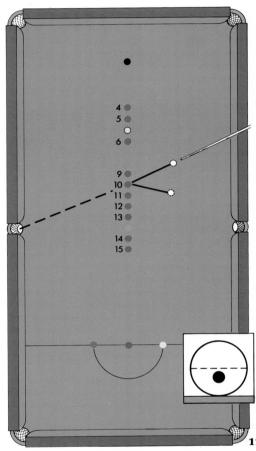

your options narrowing later on. Being almost straight on Red 8 is a happy accident, because you can pot it without disturbing a red either side. But while Red 8 may be the clear choice of pot, there are two alternative ways to play the shot. You can screw back for the pink into the top right-hand pocket, or run through for the pink into the top left-hand pocket. Your choice should be governed by the fact that you will want to be between three-quarter ball and straight on the pink, both for potting ease and so as not to cannon into other reds.

Once you realize that, your choice is made for you. If you screw back, you must be accurate with your screw to about 2½ balls' width, to get the desired angle. If you run through, you have almost double that margin. If to gain that safety margin you had to accept a more difficult pot on the pink, you would have to weigh the respective advantages and disadvantages very carefully, but in this case there is not much in it. Run through Red 8.

8 Pot the pink (three-quarter ball or a

little fuller) with gentle screw, aiming to be more or less straight on Red 4. This is a fairly easy positional shot, but it is the longest pot to date.

9 A change of plans here. There is nothing whatever wrong with Red 4. Just a matter of potting it and running through for the black into the right-hand pocket. But look at Red 7. It is just as easy to pot it into the middle. Given the way things stand now, Red 7 might prove slightly more awkward at a later stage (just an experienced hunch, really). The lesson here is that

The line-up

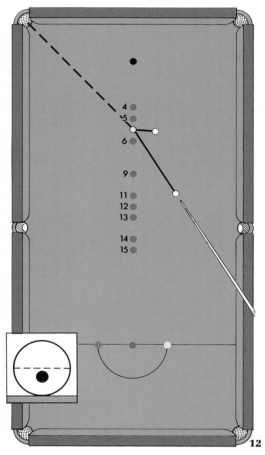

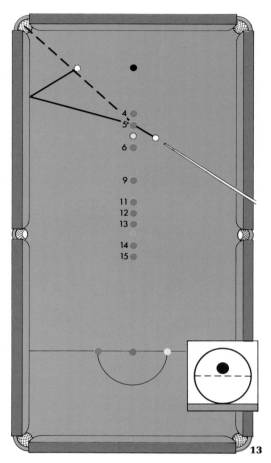

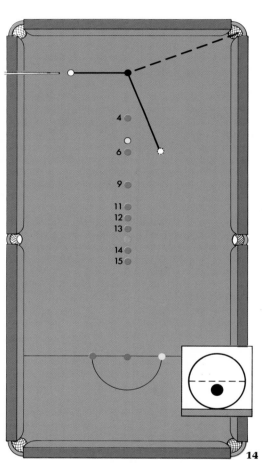

even when you get perfectly into position as intended (in this case on Red 4), always survey the table to see if you have actually left yourself an even better shot. Do not try to adhere rigidly to any plan in break-building. Be flexible, always responding to the pattern of the balls. Red 7 is three-quarter ball or a little fuller. A gentle screw shot should bring you straight on the pink. Be careful not to leave yourself short. Even an inch short of straight on the pink would necessitate the use of the rest. It is better to risk going a little too far rather than

have that happen.

10 Perfect on the pink, leaving a choice of run-through or screw for the next position. Run-through is dangerous because you would need to be inch perfect. There is never much of a margin when you get in so close amongst the balls. You want a bit of elbow room, so screw back off the pink. That is bound to leave you with ample choice. However, guard against excessive use of screw, which would bring you uncomfortably near the side cushion.

11 Note that the cue ball has not screwed back dead on line (easy to see in this case once the pink is re-spotted). The nap of the cloth has caused it to fall away slightly, a matter of no consequence in this instance but a factor you should be aware of. Sometimes it is of consequence. Choices now abound, but Red 10 is best. It is just off straight into the middle pocket, but not sufficiently so to cause the cue ball to cannon into a neighbouring red. Here again, you can either run through or screw back (for the pink in either case). Run-

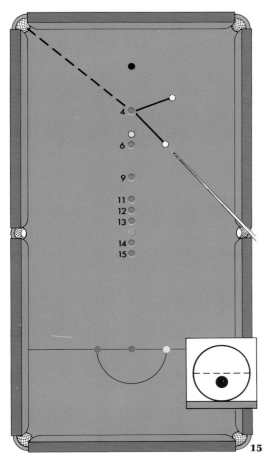

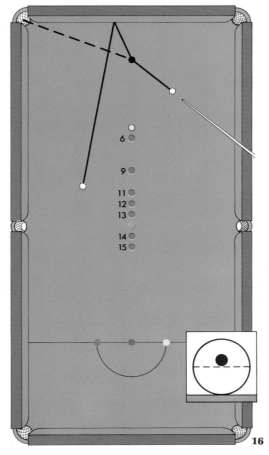

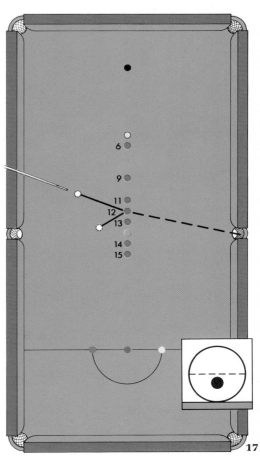

through would leave a longer and therefore more difficult pink. Screw is the better choice.

12 A three-quarter ball angle on the pink is fine. A gentle screw will leave you on three reds (4, 5 and 6). Ideally, Red 5 would be best because it would open a gap.

13 Red 5 it is (three-quarter ball), although there is no way of holding the cue ball for ideal position on pink into the middle. Therefore you must be looking for the black. You could

run through gently for it, but there are distinct advantages to playing more boldly. Play the shot with sufficient strength to bring the cue ball off the side cushion, up towards the black. It makes for a much easier black.

14 The second advantage to playing Red 5 that way can now be seen. The cue ball is so positioned that the top cushion will not have to be used in this shot – and it is the most demanding shot yet. The three-quarter ball angle on the black will bring the cue ball down the table, which is what

you want. You could play it plain ball, but if you did you would need perfect strength to bring the cue ball off the side cushion and nicely on to a red. That is always the difficulty with plain ball, the need for perfect strength. There are plenty of places along that plain ball path where you would find yourself in a real mess. Screw is the answer, but here again you have to get it right. If you screw too much, you might cannon into Red 4 (ideally, your next pot). If you screw too little you will finish up close to the side cushion.

The line-up

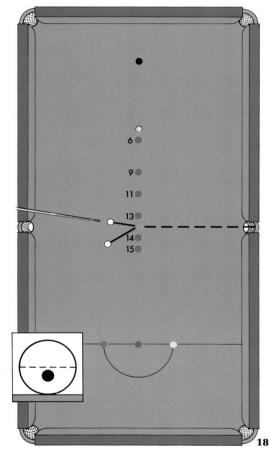

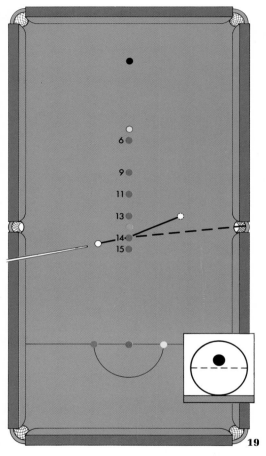

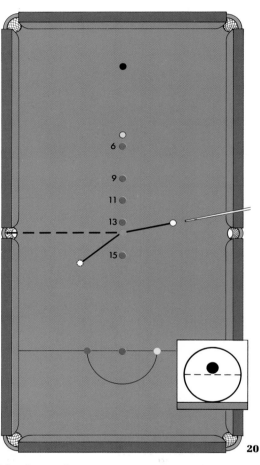

15 The three-quarter ball angle on Red 4 is fine. Now, however, it is time to take stock. The low- and middle-numbered reds have been disappearing nicely, and there are plenty of useful gaps between those remaining. It is about time to open up some space around the blue spot. If you leave all those high-numbered reds to the end, one bad positional shot could easily end the break, because you would have nowhere else on the table to look for a loose red that might let you rescue the situation. For as long as possible, you want to keep your options

open. Now is the time to prepare for some work around the blue spot. You must pot Red 4 and get on to the black. This time, however, you want to leave yourself nearer half-ball than three-quarter ball on the black. That way you will not need such weight of shot to bring the cue ball off the top cushion and down to the middle of the table. But you do not want to be too thin on the black because that would endanger the pot. A gentle screw shot on Red 4 should do the job.

16 The near half-ball angle on the

black is what you wanted. It is best to play it plain ball, because if you apply too much screw you could end up close to the side cushion. Plain ball with a hint of top is perfectly safe. There are no reds in the way and the cue ball is certain to miss the pink and end up decently positioned somewhere in the centre of the table.

17 Both Red 11 and Red 12 are on, but Red 12 is better for two reasons. It opens a gap and from it you should be able to screw back to get almost straight on the blue.

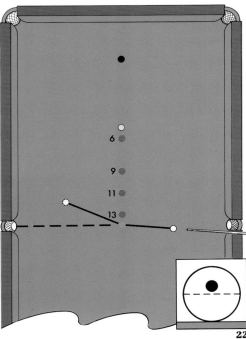

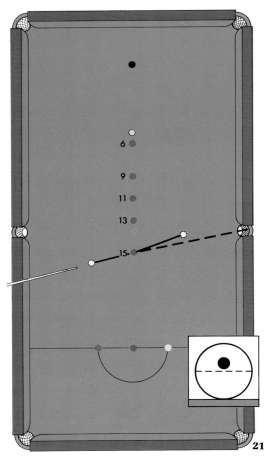

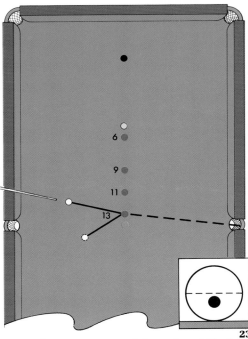

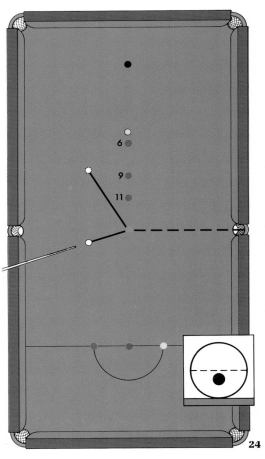

22 Roll in the blue (pocket weight, just enough to get it there), which leaves you just off straight on Red 13.

18 The blue is almost straight. Screw back for choice of Red 14 and Red 15.

19 You are now perfectly positioned to clear up all the reds around the blue spot, before going back up the table to finish the job. Pot Red 14 and run through for a nearly straight blue.

20 Pot the blue and run through to leave yourself on Red 15.

21 Pot Red 15 and run through to leave an almost straight blue. It is vital to keep to the baulk side of blue.

23 The important thing about Red 13 is that you must, following the pot, leave the cue ball to the baulk side of the blue, so that when you pot the blue you will come on to Red 11. You can either run through Red 13 to be one side of the blue, or screw back to be the other. There is nothing in it.

24 Having screwed back slightly baulk side of the blue, screw the blue into the side pocket, hoping to get on Red 11. If you fail to get nicely on Red 11, you will have Red 6 into the right-hand corner.

The line-up

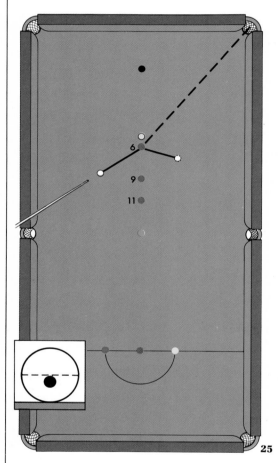

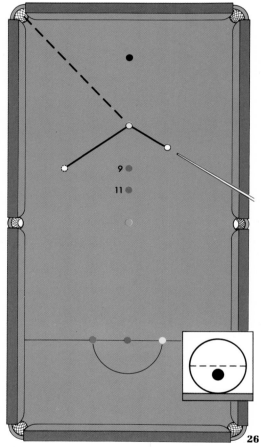

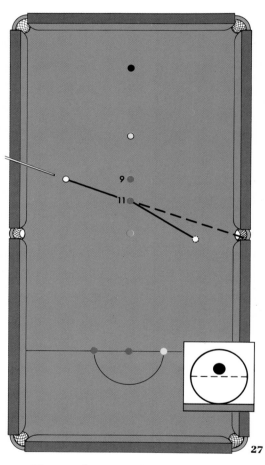

25 Red 11 and Red 6 are both on, and both at the favourable three-quarter ball angle. On reflection, there is nothing whatever to choose between them, so for variety's sake it is reasonable to switch to Red 6. Play a stun shot on Red 6, taking care to leave the cue ball slightly up table from straight on the pink. That is, ensure that you have something like a three-quarter ball angle to your right. If you leave a three-quarter angle to your left, you will in the course of potting the pink take the cue ball away from the remaining reds.

26 Pot the pink with gentle screw, with the intention of leaving yourself with either a three-quarter ball angle on Red 9 into the top corner or a three-quarter ball angle on Red 11 into the middle.

27 The angle on Red 11 is fine, but it is critical that the cue ball should end up on the baulk side of the blue. Otherwise, in potting the blue you will send the cue ball away from Red 9. It would be a pity to break down now! Run through Red 11.

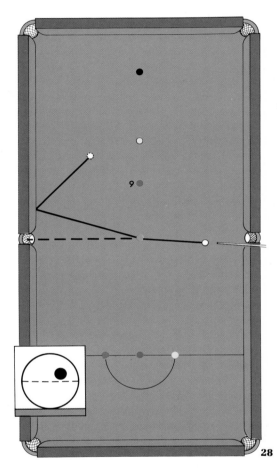

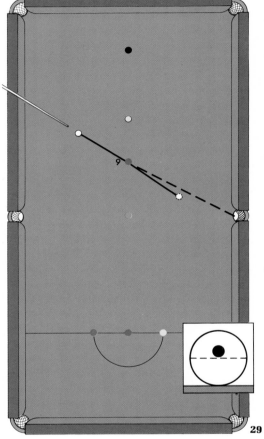

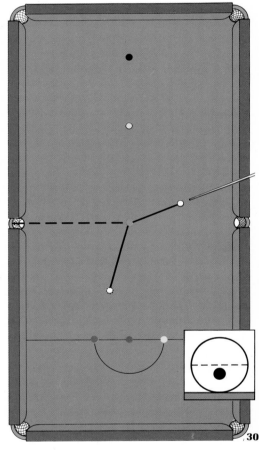

28 Pot the blue and run through with right-hand side off the side cushion for Red 9. Note that this is the first and only use of side in the course of a thirty-shot sequence. Not quite typical, perhaps, but it indicates how close-range work depends so heavily on simple little screw, stun and run-through shots to the exclusion of side. You must always have a good reason for using side. In this case, running side brings you closer to the final red.

29 This position is pretty well ideal for clearing the table. Being almost straight on Red 9, you are able to run through for the blue. The blue leads you naturally on to the yellow. Red 9 should be played plain ball with a hint of top, and the weight is critical. You want the cue ball slightly up table from the blue. Not too much up table, because that would make it difficult to pot the blue and hold the cue ball for the yellow. Not straight on the blue, because that would make it impossible for you to get any closer to the yellow than the line running be-

tween the middle pockets. Worst of all would be to get baulk side of the blue. That would take the cue ball away from the yellow.

30 Pot the blue, using soft screw to come straight on to the yellow.

Having come this far, you should have little difficulty in mopping up the colours!

Looking ahead

When on television you watch a really big break – a century clearance, say, or on very rare occasions even a 147 – you might be tempted to think that the player has planned the break at least in outline before potting the first red. He has not. It would be beyond human capacity to plot that far ahead, and in any case it would be meaningless to make the attempt because it is impossible to pot with such positional accuracy as to follow any scenario for thirty shots or more. What a good player does do, however, is assess the lie of the table, and relate it to the stage of the game. He can see that the reds are nicely positioned for a productive spell around the black spot, or that in the course of snapping up two loose reds he must open the pack in order to continue the break, or that a particular ball must be developed from an unpottable position, and so forth. More immediately, he must always look at least two shots ahead. That is, before he pots one red, he not only must have clear positional intention for the colour to follow, but similar designs on the next red. That is the only way of fashioning a substantial break. Forward planning, therefore, really comes down to selecting the shot (often from a choice of many) that best furthers your aim of monopolizing the table and therefore the scoreboard.

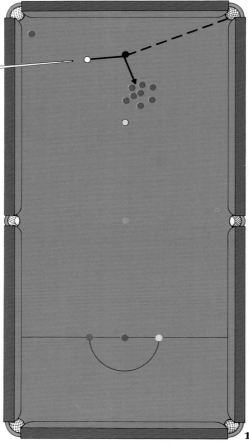

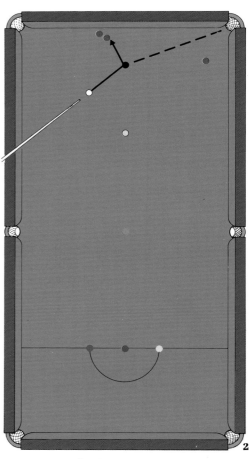

1 This three-quarter ball angle on the black is ideal for disturbing the pack. And now is the time to do it, because you have an easy red as insurance should the pack not open in a favourable way.

2 Being a little more than half-ball on the black, it is relatively easy to stun into the unpottable reds, which should with any luck run into such position that a total clearance is at least a possibility.

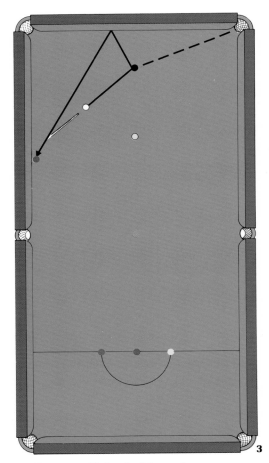

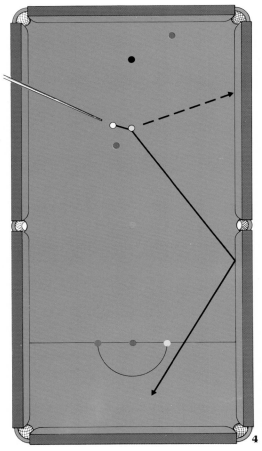

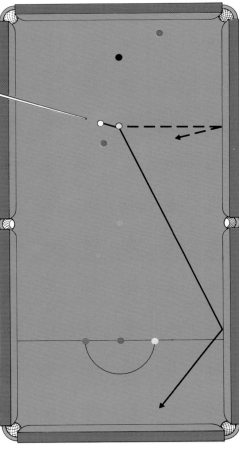

3 Screw off the half- to three-quarter ball black so as to dislodge the last remaining red from the side cushion.

4 You have potted a red but failed to gain good position on a colour. Suppose you are forty points ahead. All you need worry about is letting your opponent in with a winning clearance. You want, therefore, to play a safety stroke on the pink in such a way as to leave the pink tight on the side cushion (and thus unpottable – an obstacle to a clearance.)

5 This is an identical situation to 4, except that in this case you are forty points behind. Now it is you who needs the total clearance, and therefore you will want to play a safety stroke on the pink in such a way as to leave it in the open. That way, if your safety stroke forces an error from your opponent the table is at least theoretically at your mercy.

The break of the championship

The essence of successful break-building is to play each shot in such a way as to make the following one as easy as possible. The more difficult any particular pot is, the greater the likelihood that the break will come to an abrupt end. That is self-evident theory, and as you gain skill at positional play you will automatically apply it to the best of your ability. Your success at snooker depends upon it.

In reality, however, things often work out quite differently. Either you are faced with a difficult shot from which the positional outcome is dubious, or you make a positional error. It happens all the time, at any level, and when it does you either have to adopt safety tactics or accept the challenge of a difficult pot. The particular circumstances of the frame (or match) will affect the choice, but you will often have seen the professionals take on a difficult pot and make it only to leave themselves facing another, and take that on successfully, only to leave themselves with yet another difficult pot, and so on. To fashion a break in this manner puts enormous strains on anyone's potting ability, particularly under matchplay conditions. The following sequence has entered snooker history as being quite remarkable.

In the 1982 Embassy World Championship semi-final, Alex Higgins stood on the brink of defeat. He had played very well but Jimmy White had played brilliantly to lead him 15-13. From this position, two down with three to play, Higgins retrieved one frame with a break of 72, but White led 59-0 in the next. White

therefore needed only to pot three more balls to leave Higgins needing a snooker. He had been potting everything, but after an opening break of 41 he had missed a routine black, and now at 59 he missed a red using the rest. Had he potted that red, his excellent position on the pink would virtually have guaranteed him a place in the final. Even as it was, the odds were that he would still get at least one more chance to clinch frame

Higgins and White shake hands during their semi-final contest. It was an epic struggle – completely draining the two competitors

and match, because there was an unpottable red just baulk side of the middle pocket.

Higgins has an enviable habit of playing well when his back is to the wall, but this really was a desperate plight, to put it mildly.

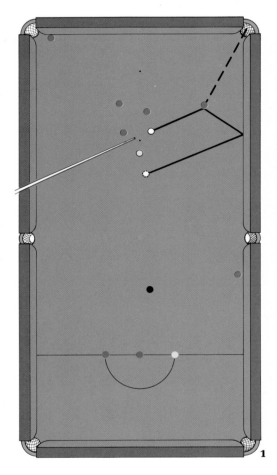

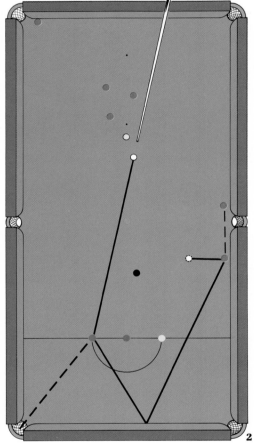

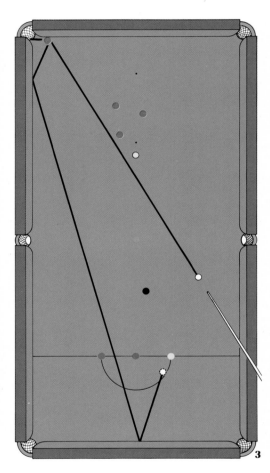

1 Initially, the only pottable red was one to the right-hand corner. In potting it, Higgins completely misjudged the strength of his shot and left himself short on the pink when virtually any position on the left-hand side of the table along the line the cue ball was travelling would have left an easy pink. The blue was not only a very difficult pot, with the intended pocket out of vision, but it offered no subsequent position without an exceptional shot.

2 Higgins could have played a safety shot as there were just enough reds left to win without the aid of snookers, but deciding that the time had come for do or die measures he swept in the long green – knowing that if he missed it he had almost certainly played his last shot. By a curious irony, having been forced into this deep trouble by missing position on the pink, he had, in fact, the angle on the green that allowed him to develop the awkward red into a pottable position.

3 Meanwhile, the only pottable red was a thin cut to the left-hand corner pocket, which made it difficult to control the speed of the cue ball. If the cue ball had rebounded out of baulk he would have had a choice of black into the middle pocket or one of the baulk colours. Instead, it finished within the 'D' without leaving the angle he wanted on any of the baulk colours in order to get the cue ball up the table for the next red.

The break of the championship

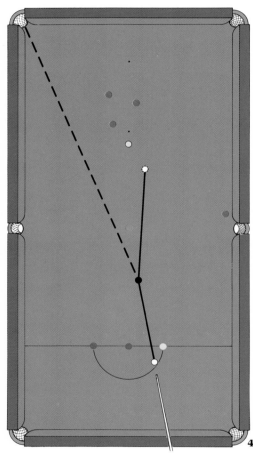

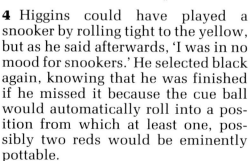

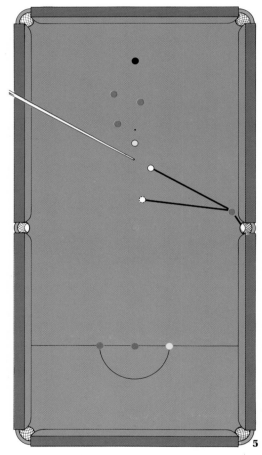

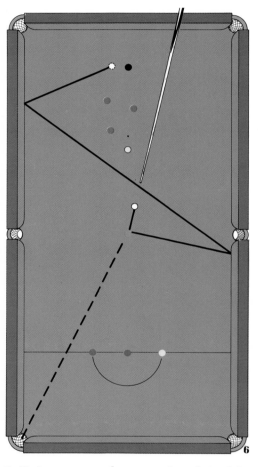

4 Higgins could have played a snooker by rolling tight to the yellow, but as he said afterwards, 'I was in no mood for snookers.' He selected black again, knowing that he was finished if he missed it because the cue ball would automatically roll into a position from which at least one, possibly two reds would be eminently pottable.

5 Concentrating fiercely to pot the black, he did not run the cue ball quite far enough for what would have been his preferred red, the one slightly left-most in the diagram, although he knew of course that the red nearest the middle pocket would be pottable virtually wherever the cue ball finished past the blue spot. This red, however, did require quite a delicate snick, and not too much pace could be used. When potting at an acute angle into the middle pocket the ball can only enter it off its jaws, and excessive pace will therefore cause the ball to jump out.

6 Being somewhat restricted in his positional options, Higgins played to leave himself on the blue, but not at the angle at which he finished. Undaunted, he produced the shot of the break, potting the blue with screw and extreme left-hand side. The latter caused the cue ball to spin very sharply off the side cushion, and travel back up the table towards the reds. He actually hit this shot 'too well'. His intention was to leave the left-most red to the right corner pocket, but the cue ball travelled too far.

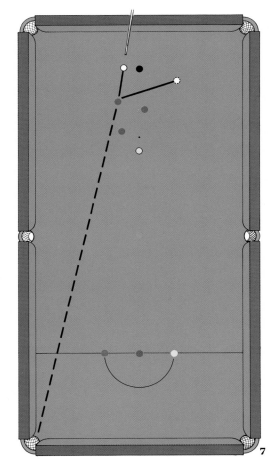

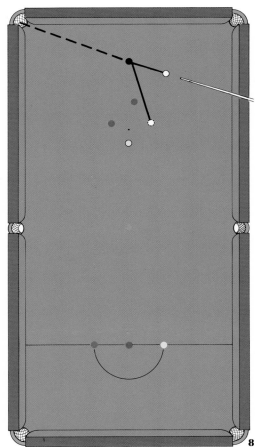

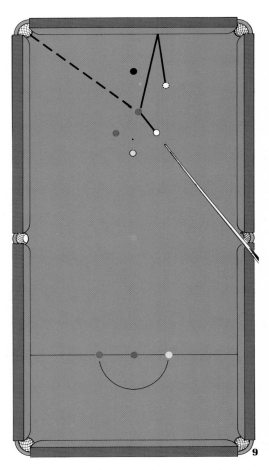

7 Another difficult pot, piling on the pressure. He made a beautiful long red to the baulk pocket and screwed across for the black, prime position at last.

8 Now a straightforward black from its spot, screwing out for one of the loose reds.

9 He potted the penultimate red with the rest, bouncing the cue ball off the cushion for the black.

The break of the championship

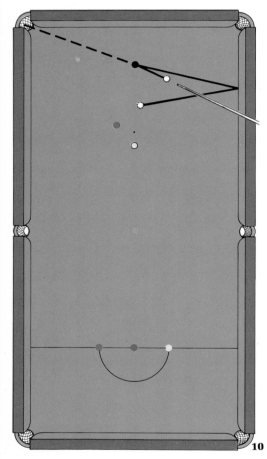

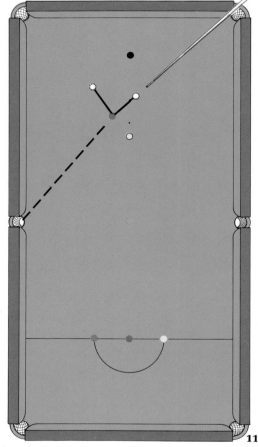

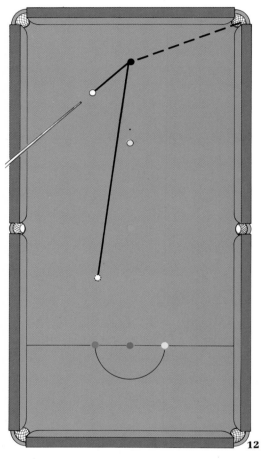

10 A half or three-quarter ball angle on the black would have made it easier to get position on the last red, but from straight on the black he screwed back off the side cushion to leave the last red to the middle.

11 He stunned the last red into the middle pocket, taking care to leave the kind of angle on the black that makes it easy to get on the yellow.

12 By now Higgins had done all the hard work, and that in itself imposes a special kind of pressure because the player now knows that he cannot be defeated by the difficulty of the situation, only by his own frailty. Mercurial though he may be, Higgins tends to be very reliable in these circumstances. From the black, he played the cue ball off the top cushion with a touch of left-hand side into perfect position on the yellow, with the colours on their spots (except the pink, which was still in good position).

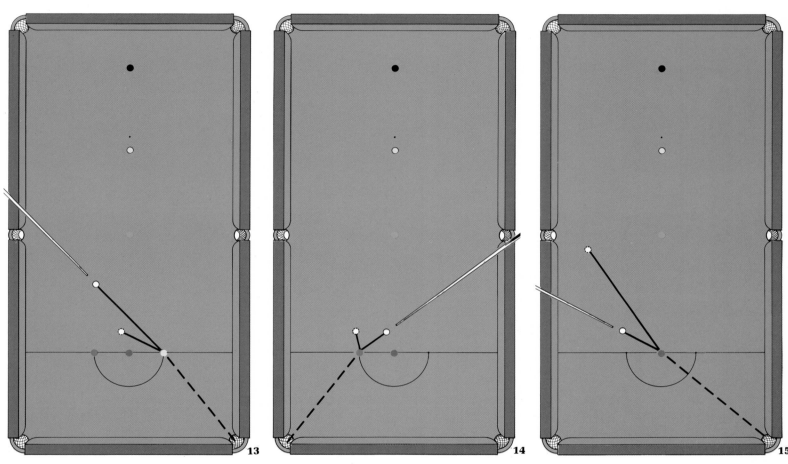

13 The yellow was just a shade off straight, but it was an easy matter to screw for green.

14 From point-blank range he potted the green, screwing gently for brown.

15 From the three-quarter ball brown Higgins screwed directly back for the blue.

The break of the championship

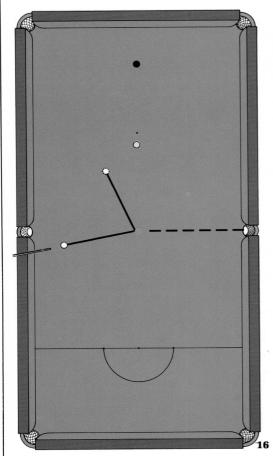

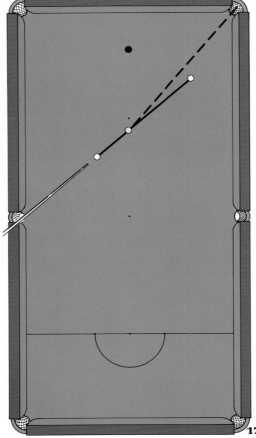

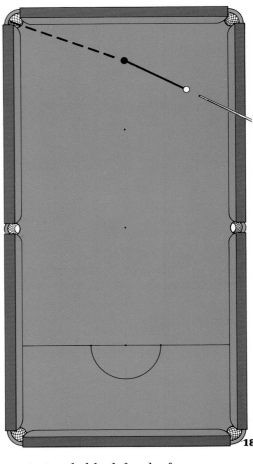

16 The pink was a bit below its spot and the table running very fast, so it would have been dangerous simply to roll the blue in because the cue ball could have finished awkwardly on the pink. Instead, he screwed sharply back to leave himself a straight pink.

17 He potted the pink with ease.

18 A simple black for the frame.

Summarizing for the BBC, John Spencer described this clearance as 'the break of the Championship'. No one argued. It brought Higgins level at 15-15. He then won the final frame and went on to defeat Ray Reardon 18-15 in the final.

Alex Higgins in full flow (above) is a compelling sight. He virtually sprints around the table, selecting shots instantaneously and throwing himself into them like a man possessed

Having disposed of White in the semi-final, Higgins went on to defeat Ray Reardon in the final to claim his second world championship. His delighted young family shared in the emotional celebration following his victory

Safety play

Safety play becomes an increasingly important aspect of the game as your standard of play improves. At the pinnacle of the game it is as significant as potting, and you will frequently have been absorbed by the nail-biting spectacle of two great players engaged in a desperate battle of wits as they try to deny each other a potting opportunity. At the other end of the scale, the complete novice has little incentive to consider safety play, except when he is presented with an obvious opportunity. His opponent, assuming he is of roughly equivalent standard, will not be so dangerous as to justify making his life unduly difficult. He is not going to amass a winning break just because you have let him in. Conversely, if by playing a safety stroke a novice subsequently gets a favourable position himself, he is unlikely to be able to capitalize on it in the way that a more experienced player can. The novice is therefore advised to concentrate on potting and break-building, leaving the subtleties of safety tactics to a later stage, when the need for them will be readily apparent. It is disheartening to see novices engaging in grim safety battles when they should be developing potting skills.

There are a few situations that obviously dictate a safety stroke,

John Virgo is forced to bridge awkwardly, as he attempts a safety stroke near the top of the table

Tony Knowles is facing a difficult safety stroke from the baulk cushion

where there is nothing pottable, for instance, or when you need snookers to win. Beyond that, there are no hard and fast rules. The lie of the balls, the state of the game, or the match, the player's feeling of confidence, or lack of it – all these factors must influence the decision whether to attempt a pot or play for safety. It is a question of weighing the odds. What are your chances of making the pot, the way you are feeling at that moment, and, if you do make it, is it likely to bring significant profit? If you miss it, what are you likely to leave your opponent? If you opt for safety, can you leave your opponent in real difficulty, preferably snookered?

Aggressive safety shots

Leaving your opponent in deep trouble should be the goal of all safety play. It is not good enough to adopt a purely negative approach – spoiling tactics designed just to keep your opponent from scoring. Snooker is a game of initiative, and safety play should be viewed as a means of keeping or seizing the initiative. A positive safety shot is one that attempts to stretch your opponent to breaking point. It is one that tries to leave him with such a difficult shot that he is likely in his turn to leave you with a scoring opportunity. Aggressive safety play is an attempt to make openings. The most aggressive safety shot of all is the deliberate snooker, preferably one of fiendish difficulty. However, leaving the cue ball tight against a cushion with the object ball the length of the table away and not near a pocket is suitably hostile.

Players sometimes adopt safety tactics with an ulterior motive. Finding themselves hopelessly behind in a frame, they nevertheless persist in laying snookers in an attempt to disturb their opponent's potting rhythm. In doing so they hardly improve their own potting rhythm, but if they are feeling out of touch in any case they may feel that they have little to lose.

It is important not to make a fetish of safety play. Treat it as an important aspect of attacking snooker, not as a substitute for it. By all means use it to demoralize your opponents, but not simply to bore them. Your general maxim should be not to use safety for safety's sake, and when you do use it, to do so to the most telling effect.

It would be possible to fill several books with examples of safety tactics, but even then it would only be by chance if some of them directly mirrored actual positions you will face on the table. Such is the infinite variety of snooker. You should, however, find the principles explored in the following examples directly relevant to your own tactical play.

Breaking off

The wide exposure of televised snooker has (mercifully) curbed the appalling practice of playing a power shot on the break-off. Even novices now realize that scattering the pack on the opening shot, presumably in the hope of fluking a red, makes a mockery of the game. Almost as foolish, because of its negativity, is the attempt to roll gently into the back of the pack off the top cushion. The player following simply has to return the cue ball to baulk off the top cushion, leaving things more or less as they were before the opening shot. The break-off is a safety shot, and like all safety shots it should be played in a positive manner. If you win the toss, take the opportunity to seize the initiative right from the start.

Dennis Taylor has just broken off. The back reds are spreading out, while the cue ball is on its way to the top cushion — from where it will return to baulk off the side cushion

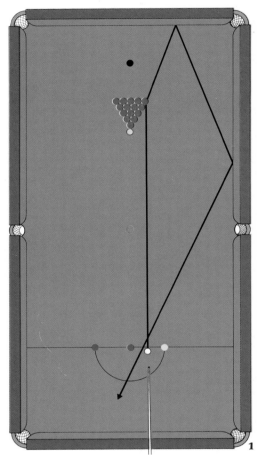

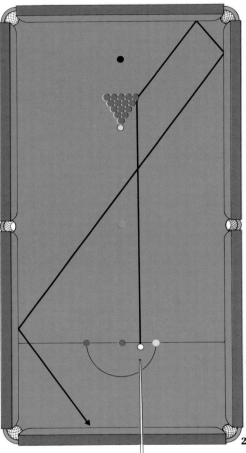

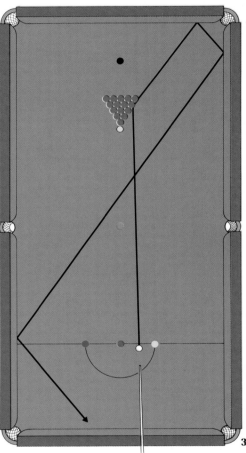

1 Only novices should break off like this. Aim for the outside red in the last row, playing plain ball with medium strength to bring the cue ball back to baulk off two cushions. The problem with this shot is that the gap between yellow and brown is fairly narrow. A kiss on the brown may leave your opponent with either a potting opportunity or a good chance of being able to leave you near the baulk cushion. Few balls have been disturbed, so the second player is unlikely to be in much difficulty.

2 This is a better way to break off using the same red as 1, and it is regarded by the professionals as the most reliable break-off. Again, aim for the outside red in the last row, but play the shot with running side. This brings the cue ball off both side cushions into the baulk area (as close to the cushion as you can get it). The advantage of this shot is that once the cue ball is past the blue it should have an easy path to baulk between the green and the side cushion.

3 This is another shot favoured by the professionals. As in 2, it is played with running side, but in this case it is the outside red of the back row but one that is struck quarter-ball. The cue ball returns to baulk along roughly the same path as 2, the difference being that the last two rows of reds have been disturbed. If you play this shot perfectly it should land your opponent in more trouble than 2, imperfectly and you will leave the cue ball at the top end of the table.

Safety in the early stages

Assuming it has been a successfully executed safety shot, the early stages of a frame should consist of an exchange of safety strokes. This initial sparring continues until a realistic potting opportunity presents itself, either through an error or because the balls are positioned in such a way that it is possible to pick out a 'shot to nothing' or a plant. As a rule, safety tactics involve putting the maximum distance between cue ball and object ball(s), keeping the latter unpottable. What this means in practice, since the reds are grouped around the top of the table, is getting the cue ball into the baulk area, as close to the baulk cushion as possible. There are exceptions to this, but it is the basis of safety play. The answer to a good safety shot is an even better one. During these early skirmishes you must concentrate fully on making life so difficult for your opponent that it is he, not you, who yields the first opening.

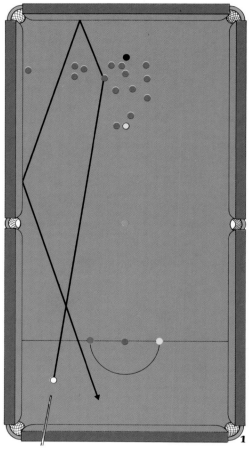

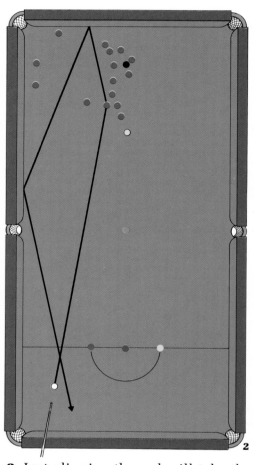

1 Moving the red into the cluster should do no harm, while the natural angle provides a simple route to the safety of the baulk area. Be careful you are not knocking the first red into others in such a way as to drift one over a pocket.

2 Just clipping the red will take the cue ball off top and side cushions towards baulk. Strive consciously not just to gauge the weight accurately enough to ensure baulk, but to leave the cue ball as close as possible to the cushion. If he has to play with the cue ball right under the cushion, your opponent will find it extremely difficult to return your safety shot with a good one of his own.

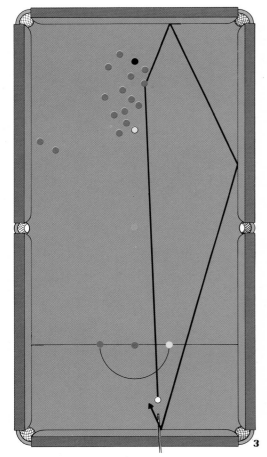

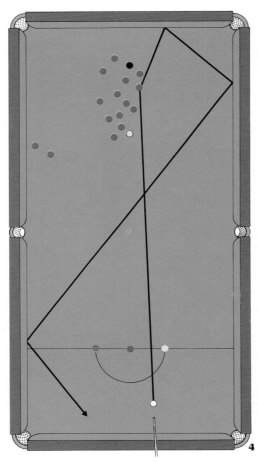

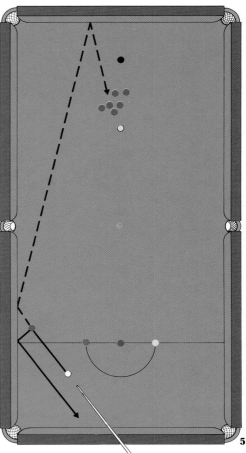

3 Clipping the outside red of the cluster is a standard safety shot, because the path back to baulk is uncluttered. But just playing thin off the red, as shown, will leave your opponent in little difficulty. See 4.

4 This is an identical situation to 3. Avoid the blue by using running side to widen the angle off the top cushion. Your opponent has a much more difficult safety stroke from this side of the table because the two reds near the side cushion are impeding his path back to baulk.

5 Bearing in mind that the basic objectives of early safety are to get the cue ball near the baulk cushion and/or behind a baulk colour, it is sometimes possible to contrive the kind of shot that sends a loose red towards the pack while screwing down to the baulk cushion with the aid of some left-hand side. To prevent the red returning to the baulk area, play for the pack to catch it like a safety net. This will also disturb a few reds slightly and make your opponent's reply more difficult.

Shots to nothing

The shot to nothing is one of the most valuable tactical weapons in a snooker player's armoury. In the early stages of a frame in particular, the player who is adept at picking them out and playing them will have a great advantage over the player who sees nothing but potting opportunities on the one hand, and safety strokes on the other. The shot to nothing is one in which a possible pot can be combined with a definite safety stroke. As a rule it means bringing the cue ball safely into baulk, thereby causing no damage should the pot be missed. If the pot succeeds, however, one of the baulk colours can be potted to initiate a break. In the professional game, successful shots to nothing are the most common means of opening the scoring. You will frequently have seen early shots to nothing seal a frame there and then. Doubles and plants (see Chapter 5) are more often than not played as shots to nothing, because of their uncertain outcome, but a great many potting opportunities you might decline can be viewed in a more favourable light when they present themselves as shots to nothing.

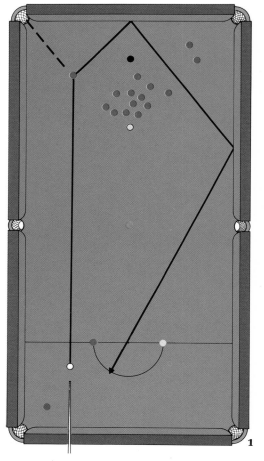

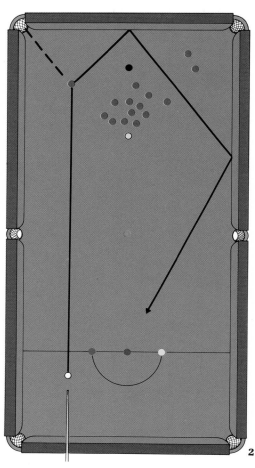

1 This is a classic shot to nothing, with the loose red so positioned that the natural angle will see the cue ball safely back to baulk off two cushions. If you make the pot you will almost certainly be on the brown so that you can pot it and get back up the table from it for your next red. If you are unlucky enough not to be on the brown you will be able to snooker behind one of the baulk colours.

2 The same shot as 1 except that, with the brown on its spot, the cue ball has to be left just short of the baulk line to give you a realistic chance of getting a break going. If a player feels positive about the red, he will do this. If he is not, he will be sure to get the cue ball back to baulk. At the worst, he will then be able to roll up behind a baulk colour. Professionals will invariably play this shot positively.

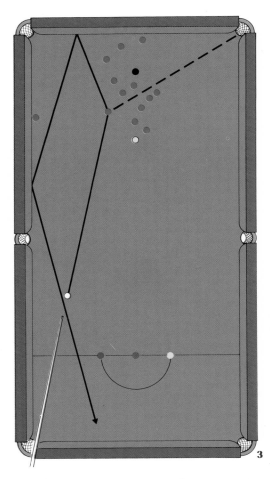

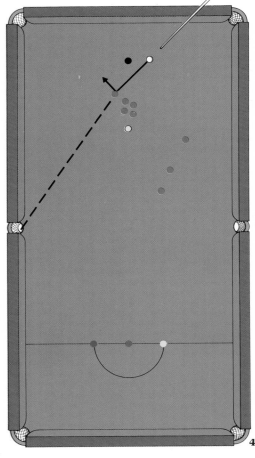

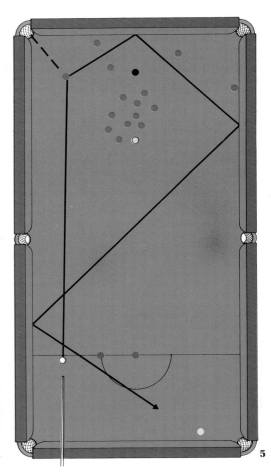

3 There is just enough room to squeeze the loose red through the corridor, while top and side cushions will bring the cue ball back to baulk. You could leave the blue to the middle pocket, but at the worst you can roll behind one of the baulk colours.

4 You have a choice of reds to the middle pocket but if you play the red to the right pocket weight to leave position on the pink, you will be certain to leave your opponent a choice of two reds into the other middle pocket should you miss. However, if you play the red to the left, as shown, stunning gently for the black, you will have prime position if you pot it and will leave nothing if you miss because the main bunch of reds will be shielding the loose ones.

5 Played with screw and right-hand side, the cue ball will run clear of the red near the top cushion, then off both side cushions to finish on the yellow. Judicious use of screw and side will create many shots to nothing.

Choice of shot

You will sometimes face situations in which you have no realistic choice of shot: you must simply take on the pot, regardless of risk, or you must attempt to reach safety by straightforward means. In the course of any frame, however, you will frequently be presented with serious choices, and choosing wisely is obviously vital to your success. Factors like risk and potential reward have to be weighed against each other all the time, while in some circumstances, especially towards the end of a frame, the score itself becomes a prime factor. You must develop the habit of surveying the table closely, rather than allowing yourself to become blinkered by obvious chances. The obvious will frequently be the correct choice, but by no means invariably so. There is no profit whatever in making hasty, impulsive decisions.

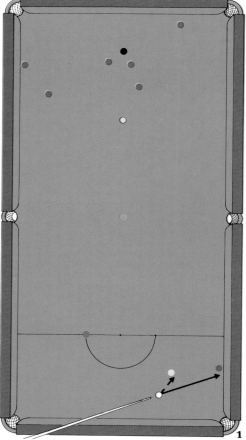

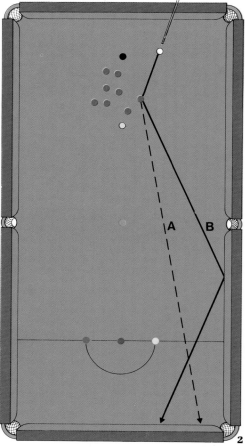

1 You have potted the red but failed to get position on a colour. You are presented with a gift snooker – simply trickle up behind the yellow. However, consider the brown instead. If you lay your snooker behind it, rather than the yellow, it will be considerably more difficult for your opponent to negotiate an escape route.

2 You want to bring the cue ball to the safety of baulk, and probably the easiest way to do that is by playing thin on the red, which will take the cue ball straight down towards the baulk cushion (A). The trouble is, even if you can leave the cue ball on the baulk cushion, your opponent should be able to return your safety shot. If you play B, however, which is half-ball contact, you put him in far deeper trouble and may actually lay a snooker behind the yellow.

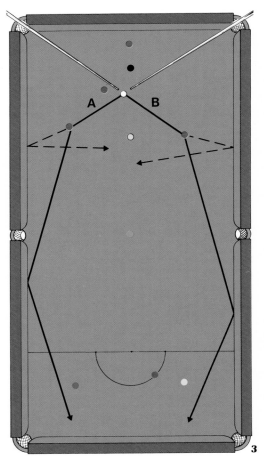

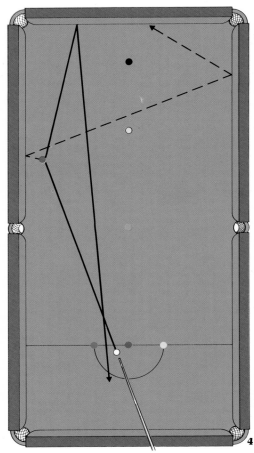

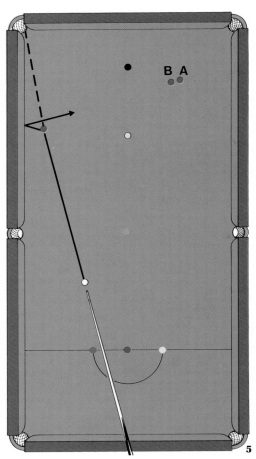

3 Sometimes, two or more reds offer a choice of safety shot. Here you can play safe off Red A with a reasonable possibility of leaving the cue ball safe on the baulk cushion behind the green. Red B, however, is the better option because the yellow and brown are virtually forming a wall. If you can get the cue ball behind it at a certain angle you have three ball-widths with which to shield the reds.

4 This is undeniably a potting opportunity, but it is one to decline. It is a bad percentage shot. If you were to miss it (and even a professional would not consider his chances better than 50:50) you might expose yourself to losing the frame. The alternative safety stroke should leave your opponent in some difficulty. It is half-ball contact, doubling the red off two cushions while the cue ball returns to baulk – ideally to the baulk cushion behind the brown.

5 If missing a pot guarantees leaving an opening for your opponent, that fact makes the shot appear more difficult than it would otherwise be. For instance, if Red B were not on the table, the pot under consideration (to leave position on black or pink) would be hazardous, and a thin contact bringing the cue ball back to safety would be advisable. With Red B in position, however, the pot looks altogether more attractive, since there is a fair chance that you will leave the intended red safe if you miss it, with Reds A and B unpottable.

Snookers in the end game

Tactical snookering is applicable at any stage of the game, but when it gets down to the final few reds or, more commonly, the coloured balls alone, the snooker plays a more immediate role. If you are behind in scoring terms by more than the cumulative value of the remaining balls, you must lay one or more successful snookers to have any chance of drawing level or winning. It is tempting for the player ahead by such a potentially decisive margin to adopt 'generous' tactics. In attempting pots, he plays the object ball pocket weight, on the theory that leaving the object ball hanging over the pocket (should he miss the pot) will virtually oblige his opponent to pot it, thereby bringing his own victory one ball nearer. This is flawed theory. If, for example, you are thirty two points ahead with all the colours remaining (twenty seven points), your opponent requires two snookers to win. If you allow him to pot yellow, green and brown, he will be twenty three behind, with eighteen points remaining on the table. If he snookers you on the blue, the five-point penalty will leave him in a position to draw level and force a tie-break. If, on the other hand, he pots the blue and snookers you successfully on the pink, the final two balls will steer him to victory. The exception to this cautionary advice is a situation in which you are ahead by a winning margin with only pink and black remaining. Then, of course, pocket weight on the pink will do nicely.

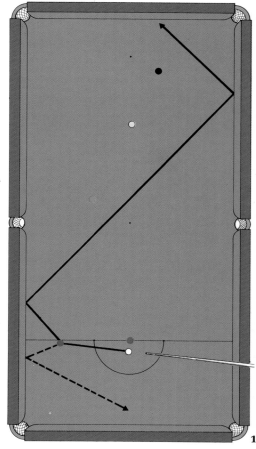

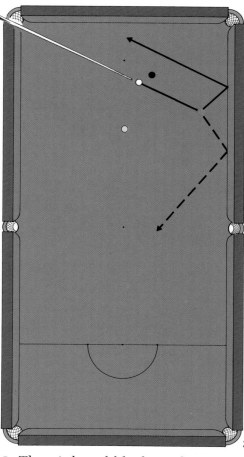

1 With the pink on its spot and the black in a helpful position, there is an excellent chance of laying a snooker behind the black. Try to get the cue ball behind the black and the green behind brown. Use a touch of running (right-hand) side for this shot.

2 The pink and black on their spots leave quite a wide area in the middle of the table to place the blue for a snooker.

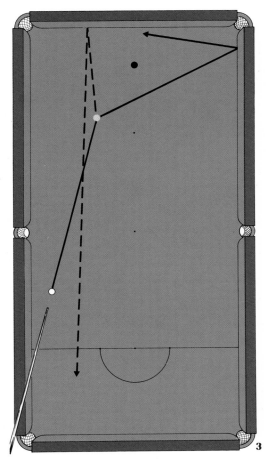

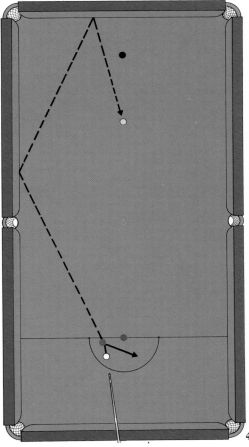

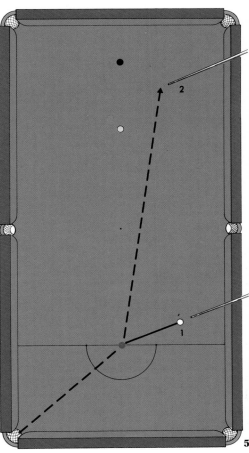

3 A three-quarter ball angle on the pink will send it to baulk, while check (left-hand) side should get the cue ball on line for a snooker behind the black.

4 You need a snooker and only the last five colours remain. A gently controlled screw shot should enable you to nestle in behind the brown, but it is even better if you can gauge the pace of the shot to leave the green as near as possible to the back of the pink. This will of course make the snooker much more difficult to hit. It will also give you every possibility of a free ball or, failing that, a chance to snooker your opponent again.

5 You need a snooker with only the last four colours on the table, but this is an instance where you should think two shots ahead. Rather than play a snooker on the brown, pot it and screw back with right-hand side to leave yourself in prime position to lay the snooker on the blue. If all goes according to plan, you will then be able simply to strike the blue full in the face, killing the cue ball dead with stun to leave it behind the pink with blue doubled off both side cushions towards baulk.

Escaping from snookers

Successfully negotiating a tricky snooker is immensely satisfying as well as important to the result. Of all the situations you will face, this one probably repays the greatest consideration. Bearing in mind that a tactical snooker has a deeper purpose than to extract a few points from you, it is vital that you do not content yourself merely with hitting the object ball. You must hit it in such a manner as not to leave your opponent a scoring opportunity (his purpose in laying the snooker). If you miss it, you must do so in a way that does no more damage than the penalty forfeit. Consequently, it may well be that the easiest or most obvious escape route is not the one to choose – a more difficult escape may be less risky overall, even if it increases the chance of a miss. A thorough knowledge of cushion angles is essential to escaping from snookers, and that can only come with experience and careful observation. There is, however, one theoretical point to bear in mind. If the object ball is out in the open, it is sound policy to play a firm shot, so that whether you hit it or not, the cue ball will travel some distance away from it (to deny your opponent an easy pot). If the object ball is on or near a cushion, play to roll up to it, because whether you hit or miss, if the balls are close together near the cushion, the object ball should be safe.

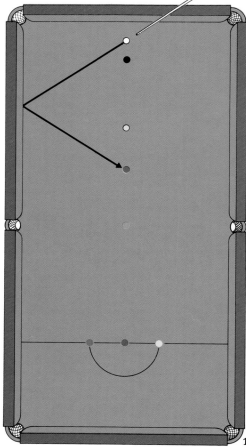

1 A straightforward escape using the side cushion. When the object ball is in the open like this, play the shot firmly enough so that if you miss it you will take the cue ball well away from the vicinity.

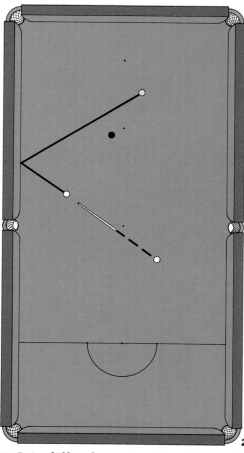

2 It is difficult to visualize the angle where the first leg is much shorter than the second. Try to imagine the angle as it would appear if the two legs were equal.

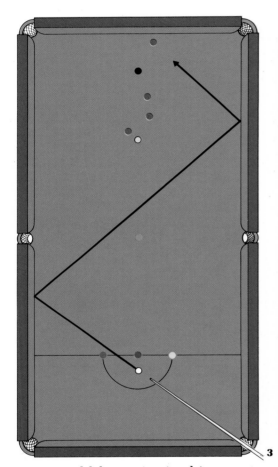

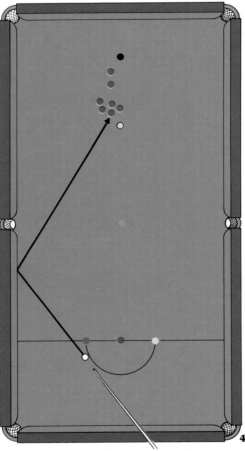

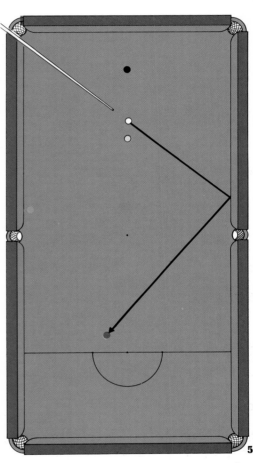

3 It would be easier in this case to aim for the cluster of reds, but you would be lucky indeed not leave your opponent with a good potting opportunity. It is better to go for the isolated red, and play with just sufficient strength to reach it. That way, even if you miss, you will not do grave damage.

4 One escape that occurs time and time again is when you are snookered behind a baulk colour with some but not all reds disturbed from the pack. Your overriding concern here must be safety. Play with dead strength just to reach the pack of reds. Remember that it is better to misjudge the angle slightly to one side – and thus give six away for hitting the pink – than to misjudge it to the other, because with two open reds your opponent will not have to be a Steve Davis to make at least sixteen easily.

5 This is a nasty snooker because the blue is covering the natural angle on one side cushion, and the middle pocket the natural angle on the other. Therefore, play it with running (right-hand) side.

Escaping from snookers

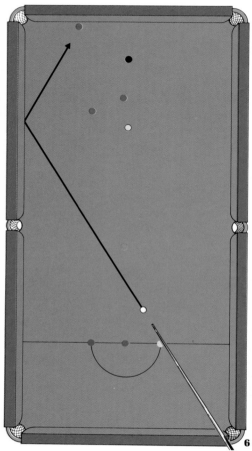 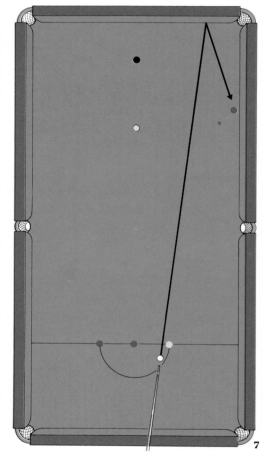 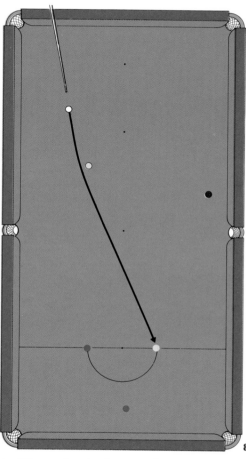

6 Whereas object balls in the open should be played at firmly, when they are on or near the cushion you should try to roll up to them, providing, of course, you are not thereby leaving another red. The aim is to leave the cue ball and object ball so close together as to make a pot impossible.

7 With practice, you should become able to escape from relatively simple snookers (where the angle is easily read) with a good chance of leaving your opponent very close to the object ball. In this case, leaving him tight against the red would contain the danger even if your opponent again put you in trouble with his next shot.

8 The principal use of swerve is in escaping from a snooker when cushion escapes are blocked.

Safety in the tie-break

Because snooker is a high-scoring game, the issue is usually decided by the time the final black disappears from the table, if not before. Sometimes, however, the frame ends all level. More accurately, the scores are tied with the table cleared, because in snooker the frame is not over until there is a winner. In these circumstances the black is re-spotted, the players toss for the first shot, and the winner of the toss (or his opponent, if that is what he chooses), plays from the 'D'. However unappetizing that first shot may appear to you, it may pay you to accept it. It is not an easy safety stroke but if it is played well your opponent can be placed in more difficulty than you were. Your own state of mind and confidence – and what you judge your opponent's to be – are relevant factors in this decision.

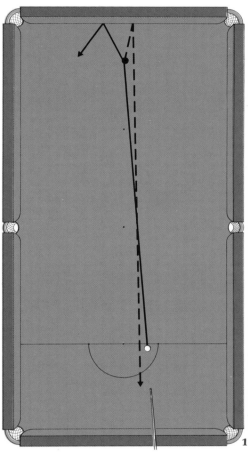

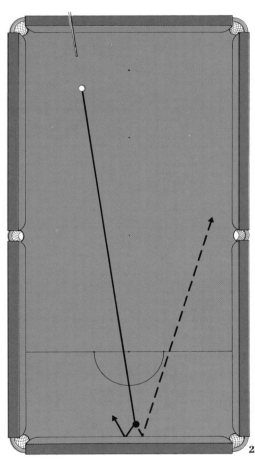

1 There are alternative ways of playing the opening shot, but this is accepted as standard procedure for attempting an uncomfortable (and necessarily tense) shot. Three-quarter ball across the black, bringing it down to baulk and leaving the cue ball at the top of the table. There are two dangers here: if you hit the cue ball too thick you risk a double-kiss; if you hit it too thin you will leave a pot to the baulk or even the middle pocket.

2 If the opening shot leaves the cue ball at the top of the table, the second shot is extremely difficult. You must bring the black safely past the middle pocket, while leaving the cue ball as deep as possible in baulk. If the black has not finished as close to the cushion as this, you can play a similar shot to 1, going across the face of the black or doubling it back over the line of the spots.

Chapter 5 SPECIAL SHOTS

For the most part you will be attempting to pot directly into a pocket. But not always. Doubling the object ball off a cushion is sometimes your best, or only, chance of keeping a break going. Alternatively, your most promising choice of shot may involve *playing one object ball on to another, with the intention of potting the second – a set or plant. Sets and plants also figure largely in those entertaining trick shot routines you may occasionally have seen. A few such trick shots appear at the end of this chapter.*

Doubling the ball

Novices tend to enjoy playing doubles, whereas professionals are chary of them. The reason for this is simple enough. The novice is not really expecting to bring the shot off, and when he not infrequently does it looks and feels a spectacular shot – particularly if he has really cracked it in. The professional has no interest in spectacular looking shots. He is invariably looking for ways to make things as easy as possible for himself and cares nothing for flourishes, everything for keeping the break going. Unlike the novice, the professional always expects to make his pots, and for the most part he will prefer not to play a double unless he can do so with small risk and the prospect of significant profit.

There are inherent problems with doubles. One is that it is unsettling to be aiming for a pocket that is completely out of your vision. As you shape up for the shot you have to imagine where the pocket is. For another, you are involved with two angles rather than the single one of a normal pot. You must figure out the angle the object ball must take off the cushion in order to reach the pocket, and then figure out the angle you need on the object ball in order to bounce it off the cushion at that angle. Finally, you have to be aware of the nature of the cushions themselves.

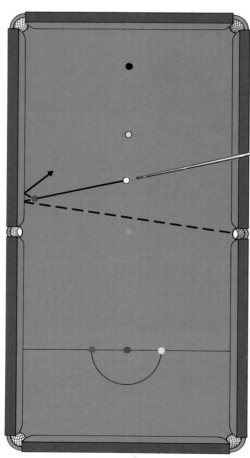

This is the most elementary of doubles, with the object ball near the side cushion and the cue ball so positioned that full-ball contact will create the potting angle

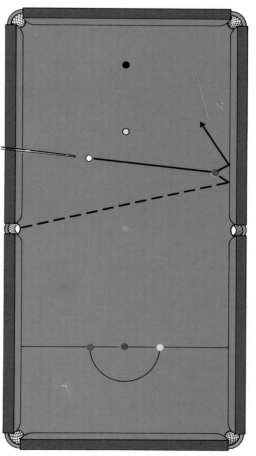

This double into the middle pocket requires angled contact. You will find it easier to discern the angle if you visualize it in reverse, from the middle pocket

If you play the shot with normal strength, the object ball will rebound at the reverse angle to that at which it arrived. If you bang the ball hard against the cushion, however, it depresses the cushion to such a degree that the angle of departure becomes unpredictably narrower. Doubles should therefore never be played hard. Some like to play them hard not just because of the satisfying effect if they go in, but because they are afraid of leaving the object ball 'on' if they miss. That is a complete mistake. If you play the shot with normal strength and fail, at least the object ball will not be sitting over the pocket. Play it as a power shot and it could go anywhere, scattering other balls around in a completely unpredictable way. Scattering balls around the table in a haphazard fashion is something the good player never does.

Having looked at the dark side of the double, especially the foolish banged one, it must be emphasized that the judicious double is a most valuable stroke to learn. Many a big break hinges, at one point or another, on pulling off a double.

Trial and error
As with potting angles, the only way you will learn to make doubles is through trial and error (preferably during practice), and by careful observation of what happens when you attempt them from various positions. Sometimes it helps to go to the intended pocket and imagine the shot backwards.

One marginal advantage the double has over normal shots is that once you

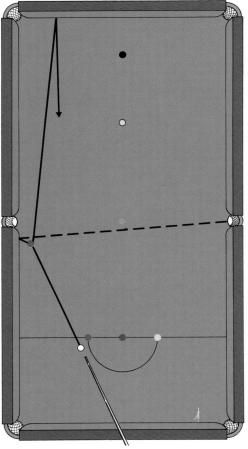

This double, played roughly quarter-ball, is risky because the pocket is partly closed, and if you miss you are likely to leave the object ball 'on'

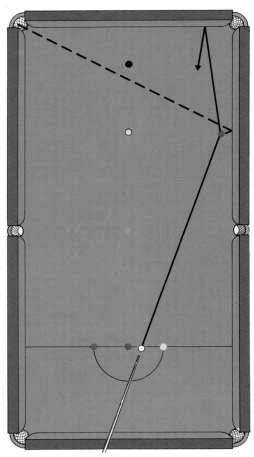

Corner-pocket doubles (here a cross-double) are risky because the pocket is partly closed and if you miss you are unlikely to achieve safety

have settled on the angle, you can give over your entire concentration to cue ball control. There is no pocket in vision to distract you. You must work on the assumption that the double will succeed (just like any pot), and therefore make certain of position. It is quite maddening to pull off a difficult double and find you have left yourself with nothing 'on'.

You should also note the fact that professionals, wherever possible, play doubles as 'shots to nothing'.

By far the most commonly played doubles (and the easiest) are into the middle pocket where the cue ball is reasonably close to the opposite side cushion. Doubles can also be played into a corner pocket, but this shot should be regarded with the

Doubling the ball

greatest of care and caution. If you miss it, the object ball has a nasty habit of wobbling about in the jaws of the pocket, to leave your opponent a sitter. Because of this danger, professionals faced with a corner-pocket double always examine the possibility of the 'cocked-hat double'.

The cocked-hat double

This could be properly described as a treble, since it involves playing the object ball off three cushions into a middle pocket. It may strike you as fanciful that you could succeed with such a shot other than by luck, but it is not as difficult as it appears (which is not to say that it is easy!) Unlike the corner pocket, the middle pocket is comparatively open. Moreover, if you miss it, the object ball will run free of the pocket, assuming you have played the shot with reasonable strength. Obviously you should never play any double at pocket weight, since that risks leaving a sitter. The snag with the cocked-hat double is that if you just barely miss it, the object ball can go in unpredictable directions. Miss it cleanly and the object ball will carry on towards the other end of the table and, presumably, safety. However, if it hits the facing angle of the middle pocket it may shoot straight back from where it came; or, it may come out of the jaws of the pocket in the direction of the opposite middle pocket. Do not, however, dwell overly on the risk factor. It is fairly rare in snooker to play a shot that carries *no* risk, which is something you must simply accept.

Finally, there is the type of double you more frequently see, and play,

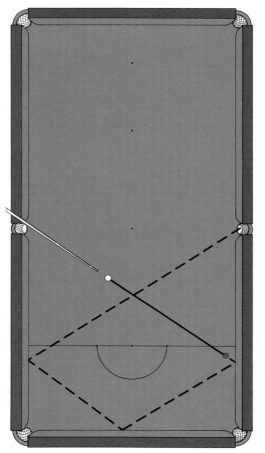

The cocked-hat double is often chosen in preference to the corner-pocket double because it is more likely to leave the object ball safe in the event of a miss

as a fluke than as a deliberate shot: the double played off one of the end cushions either into a side pocket or a corner pocket at the other end. Because it is assumed to be a fluke it causes merriment, but under some circumstances it is perfectly sensible to combine the possibility of such a double with a safety stroke. If it comes off, consider it a bonus.

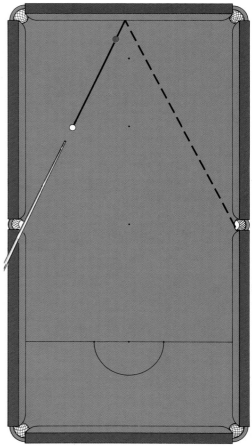

Doubling off an end cushion into a middle pocket provides little margin for error. It is therefore important to play the shot firmly enough to take the object ball well clear of the pocket in the (likely) event of a miss

Sets and plants

Television commentators have fallen into the habit of describing two slightly different types of shot under the umbrella term 'plant'. Strictly speaking, a plant is a position in which it is possible to play one object ball on to another in such a way that the second object ball will be potted. Obviously this can apply only to reds – except in free ball situations – and it really applies only to positions in which a player would actively consider taking on such a shot. Theoretically, there are plants available whenever there are red balls in the open, maybe dozens of them. Poor players, especially those who indulge themselves in really banging the balls around the table, fluke reds off plants all the time. If the two object balls under consideration are actually touching, the proper term for the position is a 'set'. For the purposes of this description the distinction between the two will be kept, although elsewhere in the book 'plant' will be used to describe both, in keeping with current usage.

Sets

The typical set is a situation in which two reds are directly in line with a pocket. It is often assumed that such a pot is unmissable – that it is, in fact, a gift shot. If ever they miss them, players assume that they were wrong in their original assessment of the situation, that the balls were not in fact in line with the pocket. In this they are more than likely to be wrong. If you take a careful look at touching balls and judge them to be directly in

Sets

line with a pocket, you are almost certainly right – right within the margins provided by the size of the pocket. How, then, can such a shot go wrong?

It can go wrong with the greatest of ease. Most of the time, you will instinctively play the first red as though the second were not there. You will, in other words, play the first against the second along the true potting line. If you do that, the second red will go straight to the pocket, every time. Sometimes, however, either from carelessness or for positional reasons, you may strike the first red entirely differently (feeling safe in your assumption that the pot is automatic). That is when you miss the pot.

The 'squeeze' effect
The term usually applied to this phenomenon is 'squeeze'. The force imparted to the first red by the cue ball, being off the potting line, is said to have the effect of squeezing the second red so that it comes off at a slightly different angle and therefore off the potting line. If the two reds are close to the pocket your error will go unpunished. The further they are from the pocket, and the slower you play the shot, the greater the deviation from the potting line. The conclusion is: when the touching balls are in line with the pocket, you must play as though you were attempting to pot the first, so as to send the second off on the true line.

Having made a mental note to heed this cautionary advice, it may occur to you that it opens up fascinating possibilities. If playing 'wrongly'

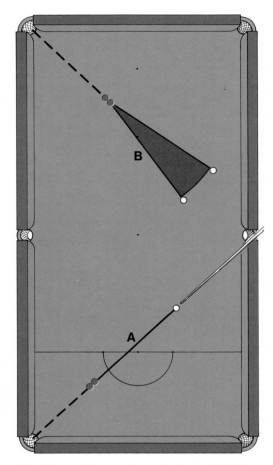

Position A is a natural set – with the touching balls in line with the pocket. In B, full-ball contact from within the shaded area should ensure the pot, but beyond it full ball will miss

can destroy a natural set, does it not follow that playing 'wrongly' can create a set where the balls are not quite in line with the pocket? The answer is that it most certainly can. That is why you see the professionals peering so intently at possible sets; they can see at a glance whether the touching balls are directly in line

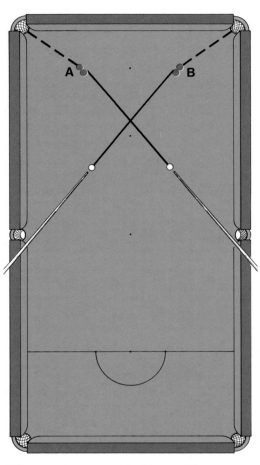

These sets are not in line with the pocket, but by striking the first object ball in A on the right-hand side, and its equivalent in B on the left, they can be pulled into line

with the pocket. What they are peering at is touching balls off line, but close to it; they are looking to create a set. By a little simple experimentation, you should be able to get a pretty fair idea of the practical limitations, and therefore uses, of this type of shot.

Before you do so, however, you

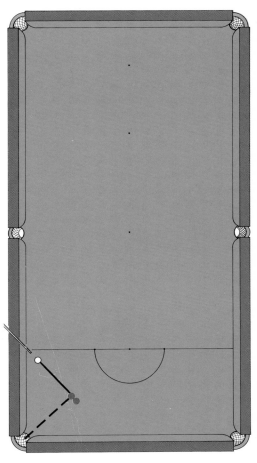

Improbable though it may seem, if the cue ball and touching balls are positioned so as to form a 'T' with the pocket, it is a natural set

must take aboard one final peculiarity about the off-true set. You would probably assume that it would work the same way as a plant does, that you would strike the first red as you would strike it were the balls a little way apart. To pull the line from right to left, for instance, you would think that you would hit the left-hand side of the first red. In reality, you do the opposite. To pull the line from right to left, you aim for the right-hand side of the first red. The further to the right you aim, the further you pull it – it is one of the mysteries of the universe.

Finally, the circumstances of a set have an effect on screw. If you play a set full ball with screw, you will discover that the screw is accentuated. It is as though you were playing into an object ball of double the weight, which means double the resistance to the forward momentum of the cue ball, which is fighting against the backspin. You must adjust your expectations of screwing distance accordingly.

Plants

If the two object balls are not touching, the set becomes a plant. The easiest plants are those in which the two reds are very close together, and both directly in line with the pocket, like a natural set. The further the reds are apart, and the further they are from the pocket, the more difficult the plant. In either case, the principle for playing this successfully is the same. You must cannon the first red into the second as though the first one were the cue ball and effectively pot the second with the first. This means the shot must be played with a very high degree of accuracy, because the slightest error or misjudgment over the contact angle on the first red will be magnified during the second phase of the shot.

Judging the angle
To judge the angle, you should address the first red as though it were the cue ball, and then try to carry the mental image of the two reds in line with the pocket with you as you return to the cue ball to select your angle. Plants are delightfully satisfying shots to bring off successfully, but initially you should resist the temptation to be very ambitious with them. There is every danger of leaving a ball 'on' if you miss, and where feasible you should consider playing them as 'shots to nothing'. And do not get so carried away with the fine calculations that you ignore positive position. You should not be taking on the plant unless you think you will get it, and there is precious little point in getting it if it merely results in your ending the break. As your confidence grows, therefore, take on the less difficult plants willingly and positively.

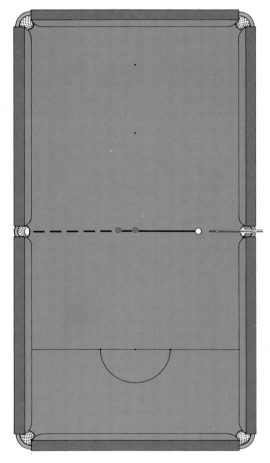

The easiest plant is one in which the two object balls and the cue ball are in line with the pocket. Simply play it full ball

As an interesting aside, it may have struck you on occasion that the Canadian professionals seem to have a particular fondness for plants, that they seem to be a little more ambitious with them than do the other players. The reason for this is that in Canada, both snooker and pool are widely played, and in their youth Thorburn and the others

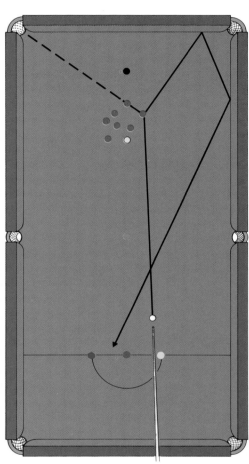

With this sort of plant you should imagine the first object ball as the cue ball in order to judge the angle

became expert at the American game. Plants, called combination shots in pool, figure largely in that game because the pockets are much bigger in relation to the balls than they are in snooker, thereby giving a greater margin of error. From this experience, the Canadians habitually see possible plants where their fellow professionals do not. All of them, however, keep

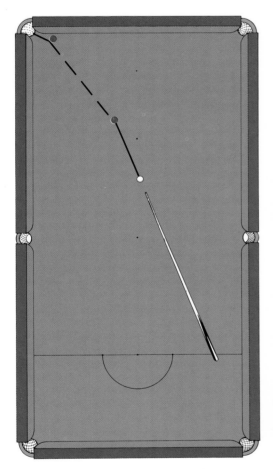

If an object ball near the pocket creates a 'wide' pocket, it increases the margins for making the pot

Tony Knowles assesses the chances of a plant – in this case one involving three object balls, which is not unusual

a beady eye out for sets and plants, and so should you.

Finally, there is an unconventional kind of plant which is really like a deliberate in-off. It sometimes presents itself when the second object ball, either red or colour, is very close to the pocket, and there is room for the first object ball either to enter the pocket direct or be cannoned into it off the second object ball. Clearly, if the second object ball is not 'on' this can be risky, but if a so-called 'wide' pocket is thus created it is there to be taken advantage of.

Trick shots

Trick shots have nothing to do with snooker proper, but occasional televised displays of them have proved immensely popular. Generally speaking, trick shot routines are featured at the end of exhibition evenings or when a one-sided match has ended long before the anticipated time. All the top players can do them, although the most widely-known and popular routines are those of Dennis Taylor, who can convulse an audience with his accompanying line in Irish gags, and John Virgo, who so delightfully parodies his fellow players.

Some trick shots are very difficult, but by no means all. The examples described below can be mastered with varying degrees of ease by the average player (one of them by a complete beginner). They are fun to practise, and of course once you have learned them you will be able to choose your moment to entertain — and impress — your friends.

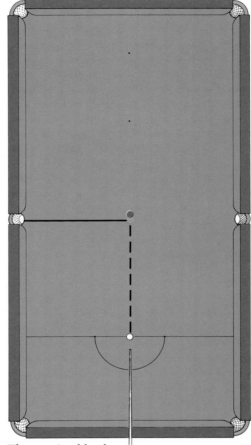

The unmissable plant

Black in the middle

The unmissable plant

If you can deliver the cue even half-way straight you will make this shot first time. As near as anything ever is, it can be described as unmissable.

Place the blue on its spot, with a red touching it in direct line with the pink and black spots. Place the cue ball on the brown spot. The three balls are now directly in line up the centre of the table. Your claim is that you can pot the blue in either middle pocket as requested — guaranteed.

To bring it off, all you have to do is strike the blue either side of centre, on the side opposite the nominated middle pocket. If you want to pot it in the left middle pocket, you can strike it anywhere at all to the right of centre (from three-quarter ball to quarter-ball — quite a margin!). Similarly, in the other direction. With the balls set up accurately, anything but full ball will result in a potted blue. Plain ball will do nicely.

Black in the middle

This is not unmissable but it is by no means difficult. Like so many trick shots it is a cunning plant that at first sight looks impossible.

The three reds and the black are all touching, and all firmly on the cushion. The fourth red is a quarter of an inch from the touching group, and a half a ball's width from the cushion. The fifth is a ball's width out

Dennis Taylor has this young lady at the mercy of his cue wizardry. Somehow he is going to fire the cue ball into the black, knocking it out of her mouth — a trick shot that never fails to extract a rapturous response from the audience (and a mightily relieved one from his selected victim)

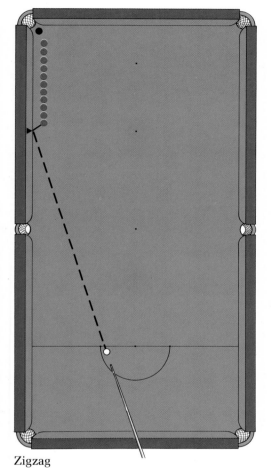

Zigzag

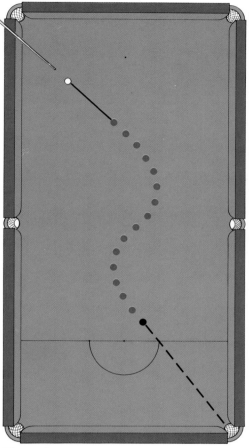

The snake

in order to find the exact point on the cushion to aim for, and since that point is absolutely critical to setting up the chain reaction you cannot be absolutely certain of bringing off the shot. If you find the shot initially beyond you, reduce the number of reds – thereby allowing you to play the shot with less power while you work out the line of shot.

The snake

This plant on the black employs all fifteen reds, and it is as easy to play off as it is exhilarating to view.

Place the balls as indicated, about three inches apart with the final red and the black directly in line with the pocket. This is a power shot, played full on the first red, plain ball. If it goes wrong you have not been sufficiently careful in setting up the snake – probably by making it excessively wriggly, which will result in too thin a contact between the reds at the extremes of the curves.

from the middle pocket.

Play the cue ball medium strength with plenty of screw. The black should go in-off.

Zigzag

This is the most difficult so far described because it is a power shot using side, but it is worth persevering with because the effect is spectacular.

Place the eleven reds and black as indicated, and the cue ball near the green spot. Play a power shot with moderate screw and right-hand side, aiming for the cushion where indicated. The idea is to come off the cushion on to the first red, cannon off the red back on to the cushion, then on to the second red, then the cushion and so on down the line, until the cue ball finally pots the black. You will have to experiment

Chapter 6 THE INNER GAME

Like all competitive games, snooker puts a heavy premium on qualities of temperament and character. More than most, it demands composure under pressure, along with decisiveness, self-discipline and courage. To a large extent, we are blessed (or cursed) with such strengths and weaknesses of character as we know we possess. What we can and *should do, however, is to adopt an approach to snooker that capitalizes on those strengths, and disguises those weaknesses. Easier said than done, of course, but start by considering the role of practice in improving your game, and therefore your chances of winning. Remember, however, that successful snooker is a pleasure, not a chore.*

Practising your game

The preceding chapters contain a number of specific practice routines, routines that have been devised over the years, mainly by professionals, first to develop and then hone the many skills needed to play good snooker. Once your game progresses beyond a rudimentary stage, which should happen quickly if you apply yourself, you will need no telling what your strong and weak points are. You will know well enough that, say, you are getting pretty useful around the black spot, but remain painfully insecure when it comes to long pots out of the baulk area. You will perhaps be able to take pride in the fact that you can screw the cue ball more or less as you intend, but the added complication of side defeats you – defeats you in the sense that what you gain in positional terms is offset by a reduction in potting accuracy. You will, for the sake of argument, have fallen quite easily into the various techniques for awkward bridging around the cushions, yet fear the rest like the plague. Most important of all, you will know whether your cue action is dependable, requiring only periodic monitoring, or whether it is erratic,

never safely left to its own devices but always needing conscious scrutiny.

As with any skill, to achieve your full potential at snooker you must accept the need to practise. Even if you have no ambitions beyond playing competently with your friends, you will find practice rewarding. If you want to progress much beyond that, you will find it essential. The top professionals vary considerably in the importance they attach to practice as far as their own game is concerned. More accurately, they vary considerably in the amount of practice they find appropriate to their own needs. But of course all the top professionals practise regularly.

Why the pros keep practising
They must do so for two reasons. First, even the best of them strive continually to get even better – Steve Davis, for instance, practises like a demon, convinced that there are areas of the game where he can still improve. The second reason is even more important. They must practise to *remain* as good as they are. It is through practice that they iron out technical imperfections that keep creeping in to threaten their consist-

ency in matchplay. They cannot afford to shrug their shoulders when they lose form for some reason or other. They must discover the reason and cure the fault.

Realistically, your experience of practice will be different from theirs, even if your approach should be the same. If you have the chance, you should practise as much as you can as a beginner. That way you will avoid getting bogged down at the most rudimentary level of play. The game is a great deal more enjoyable if you play at least to a reasonable standard. However, even if you wanted to, you probably do not have the opportunity to put in several hours of practice a day, day after day. And even if you did, such a routine might bore you quickly. Be commonsensical about it. What are your ambitions in the game? If they really are to beat Steve Davis, then you will have to approach it with the awesome single-mindedness that he has possessed since youth (and it would help if you possessed his brilliant natural ability as well). If your ambitions are more modest than that, tailor your practice to suit.

Suppose you like to play with

friends, a few times a week. Try to set aside perhaps an hour a week for practice, either on your own or with a friend. Then make that practice session really concentrated. Work consciously on those aspects of the game that most trouble you. And vary your practice so as to maintain a high interest level. Never practise the same shot over and over again to the point of tedium. Tie your practice sessions in with your actual play as closely as possible. That is, consciously apply anything you have learned at the first opportunity in a game. Try to incorporate each improvement permanently into your game, and then go back to the practice table to grapple with another difficulty. If you practise in this deliberate fashion, you will find it both enjoyable and re-

warding – it is well worth giving over a couple of frames table-time for this.

If your sights are set higher than enjoyable friendly snooker, if, for example, you are determined to make progress in the amateur game at increasingly competitive levels, the same applies. But you will have to practise more as well as play more. In that case you really will have to be ruthless with yourself in analysing your game. Like stripping down a car prior to rebuilding it, you will have to break the game down into its many component parts and work tirelessly at them. There is no other way of assembling a really formidable game, a game that will allow you to hold your own and win against increasingly skilled opposition. There are no short cuts to excellence.

Jimmy White practising 'The line-up' (see p74). Even with his great flair for the game, White must keep working on that sweetly-grooved action

The mental game

There is a world of difference between playing a friendly game in a club and matchplay, but certain key qualities of mind have a bearing on either situation. There is, in fact, a conspicuously high level of conscious mental activity in snooker. There is nothing instinctive about the game, as there is in any game with a moving ball where reactions figure largely. Every time you approach the table you are faced with a decision, or maybe a set of decisions that are interdependent. Are you going to take on the easy pot from which it is difficult to gain position, or the more difficult pot from which it is easy to gain position? If you take the easy pot and fail to get position, how will you be fixed for making a safety shot? If you take on the more difficult pot and miss it, what will you leave your opponent? At the particular stage of the game at which you find yourself, should you be viewing the situation in an aggressive or defensive light? And so on, almost *ad infinitum.*

Choice of shot is a profoundly important aspect of snooker, and of course it is entirely mental. In a friendly match, with nothing at stake, it may not feel much of a burden. The pressure of matchplay alters that, although in reality the correct choice of shot in a friendly, with all factors properly taken into account, should be the correct choice of shot in other circumstances too. It is the pressure to *make* the correct choice that is different. Time and again you will have seen the finest players visibly agonizing over choice of shot. No chess player could be weighing more finely the pros and cons (especially the cons) of various courses of action. And choose they must, either for better or worse.

Having chosen the shot, you must decide how to play it technically, and then ensure that all the technical aspects of the shot are properly performed to achieve the desired result. At a critical point in a match you will naturally be more concerned about the outcome of the shot than you would be in a friendly, and if that concern becomes apprehension, or even fear, it will be more difficult to execute the shot. You will have seen demonstrations of the killing pressure a player can be under time and again. For the spectator, it is riveting. It can make the shot almost unbearable; for some, it is actually unwatchable. Take two memorable examples. Thorburn's legendary 147 break against Griffiths in the 1983 Embassy World Championship appeared to be moving towards a triumphant conclusion as he potted the final red and prepared himself for the fifteenth consecutive black. With the black safely down, it would simply be a matter of clearing the colours from their spots. Thorburn, like all the top players, can clear spotted colours in his sleep. All he had to do was pot the black and bring the cue ball down the table to get nicely on to the yellow. In the event, he made a bit of a hash of that final black. He potted it of course, but the cue ball fell well short of his intended position. Instead of an easy yellow he faced a rather difficult one.

Cliff Thorburn had ample justification for popping champagne corks after his epic 147 break at Sheffield in 1983. He had displayed nerves of steel

Jubilation and despair – the aftermath of the 1985 Embassy World Championship final. Dennis Taylor raises his arms in triumph as the final black disappears from the table to end a titanic struggle. After such a war of nerves, a little clowning with the trophy was a natural and welcome release – for the tension-wracked audience as well. Steve Davis was gracious in defeat, but the stricken look on his face as he responds to David Vine's questions says it all. He had relinquished his title by the narrowest possible margin – on the strength of one missed opportunity under the most severe pressure imaginable

The mental game

It was not fiendishly difficult, but the cue ball was much too far from the yellow for comfort – particularly at such a tense stage. And of course the difficult pot carried a further danger. In making it, there was every chance of finishing awkwardly on the green. One of the cruel features of snooker is that drifting out of position tends to have a cumulative effect. Thorburn groaned as he saw the cue ball pull up short. His shoulders sagged. He grimaced with self-disgust. He looked for all the world as if he would have welcomed the hangman. Then he pulled himself together and made a full-blooded pot, coming perfectly on to the green. Sheffield's Crucible Theatre erupted. Thorburn's sigh of relief was echoed in front of millions of television screens. It was, under the circumstances, one of the finest shots ever played.

Two years later, in that most memorable of finals, Steve Davis and Dennis Taylor played to the ultimate death – a black ball finish in the final frame. After exchanging safety skirmishes, Taylor took on a difficult pot, missed it and left Davis with a fine cut back into the top pocket. Because the cue ball was close to the cushion and the pocket only peripherally in vision it was a more difficult shot than it may have appeared to the millions who had stayed glued to their television sets into the small hours. But it was still not that difficult for a player of class, let alone the incomparable Davis. Taylor slumped in his chair, a beaten man. Davis, quite ashen from strain as well as exhaustion, missed the pot badly, leaving Taylor with an easy pot for victory (if any pot

Alex 'Hurricane' Higgins, when at his best, channels highly charged emotions into sparkling play

could be described as easy under such trying circumstances). The crowd gasped with disbelief. Davis looked as shattered as he felt. Moments later it was all over, in a surge of jubilation around the underdog Taylor, while the stricken Davis was alone with his thoughts. Not only was and is he the most technically accomplished of players, he has earned a reputation for being mar-

vellous under pressure – every bit as good as Thorburn, and yet, on this occasion...

It would be far-fetched to imagine that you will ever shape up for a pot under such a strain as Davis endured on that occasion, but matchplay at any level creates pressures. You may be by nature good at coping with pressure or not so good, in which case you will have to discipline yourself. Even a real bag of nerves can, with effort, overcome the worst excesses of this condition.

Matchplay temperament

The word that most closely describes the ideal mental and emotional state for matchplay is composure. To be composed is not to be relaxed, let alone nonchalant. It is to be calm, calm yet alert. Players of any game who are said to have a great temperament have this ability to remain composed under pressure. They are obviously on their toes, concentrating fiercely, keyed up to a pitch that others might find unbearable. Adrenaline courses through their veins yet they remain in control, mentally and physically.

Most of the great snooker players, although not all, have excellent temperaments for the game. The most illuminating example of temperament, however, is provided by tennis. Bjorn Borg was said to have not just a good, but a perfect temperament. The interesting thing is that it apparently did not come naturally to him. As a promising junior, Borg was prone to fits of temper – tantrums, racket-throwing, the whole sorry scene that we have become accustomed to on tennis courts. After one particularly bad outburst, he was given a stern dressing down by his coach and mentor, who warned him that if he did not put a stop to such antics he could kiss his chances of success goodbye. Without self-control, he would never be a champion. Borg obviously took it to heart. His iceberg image was firmly in place by the time he arrived with a flourish on the world stage. All his furious desire

While winning the 1986 Embassy World Championship, Joe Johnson displayed astonishing composure

Matchplay temperament

to win was channelled into the controlled aggression of his tennis. His ability to remain unruffled under intense pressure is part of sporting legend. It was because of that wonderful temperament that he could win the fifth set of the 1980 Wimbledon final after losing that epic tie-break to McEnroe. Who but Borg could have shrugged off such a calamity?

It is often remarked that professional snooker, for all its pressures, is almost always played in a sporting, even gentlemanly spirit. So it is, and it is a credit to the players. There is no place in snooker for petty gamesmanship, let alone any boorish displays of bad temper or angry dissent. In any event, such is the need for utter concentration that real anger is invariably self-destructive. You cannot take your anger out on the balls, as a boxer can on his opponent, although even here it is reckoned that an angry boxer is in great peril against a cool opponent.

Cliff Thorburn would be able to confirm the shattering effects of anger, however ruefully. As well as being amongst the very finest of players, Thorburn is a true gentleman of the game. It may be, as Higgins put it memorably, that he grinds his opponents down, but he does so with unfailing courtesy and not infrequent touches of good humour, as well as with masterful technique. More than anything else, and more than anybody else in the game, he is famed for his competitive qualities – that steely concentration, that courage in adversity, the refusal to accept defeat from an apparently hopeless position, that rare ability actually to

believe the cliché about the match not being over until the conclusive ball disappears from the table. One could carry on indefinitely about Thorburn's brave fighting qualities. You will have heard such tributes countless times from television commentators and his rival players. You will have seen him salvage matches from seemingly impossible positions, almost by willpower alone. He is, in fact, the ultimate competitor, and in that sense the sporting professional *par excellence.*

An on-camera clash

Anyone who possesses such a will of iron is unlikely to be a placid person. Thorburn is far from placid. No one who has looked at that craggy face would be surprised to know that he has his share of temper. He is not on a particularly short fuse, as world-class competitors go, but he is none the less on a fuse. In a bad mood, in a darkened alley, he is not a man you would especially care to meet. And if you were playing snooker against him, you would not go out of your way to provoke him. On one televised occasion, Alex Higgins did provoke him, not intentionally, it must be said, because Higgins has far too much faith in his own genius to mess about with cheap gamesmanship. But provoke Thorburn he did.

The circumstances are irrelevant to the point of this story, but for those who did not see it (to have seen it would be to remember it), this is what happened. Thorburn was awarded a free ball after a Higgins foul, nominated it and played it. The referee called foul stroke. Some freak of

acoustics had prevented him from hearing Thorburn nominate the ball, and admittedly Thorburn had spoken on the quiet side. But his voice had carried to the live audience, and, as countless replays attested, to the television audience as well. It is therefore indisputable that his shot was perfectly legitimate, and the foul call against him a mistake. It was an injustice, and an important one because both frame and match were finely poised.

Thorburn's initial reaction was naturally one of stunned disbelief. How had he fouled? When the referee explained that he had heard no call, Thorburn immediately turned to Higgins for assistance. Had he heard? Higgins, doubtless lost in thoughts of his own, looked perplexed. For whatever mystifying reasons Thorburn's words had failed to reach the referee's ears, they had failed to reach his too.

Now had Higgins had more presence of mind, easy to say for an uninvolved spectator, he would have realized at once that Thorburn must surely have nominated the ball he had so patently played on. Moreover, it was unthinkable that Thorburn could be lying – which a false claim would directly imply. In other words, Thorburn just had to be in the right. Having grasped that fundamental, inescapable truth, the obvious response would surely have been to come to Thorburn's aid – to ask the referee to reverse his decision, which he would have done on such a request. That is what Thorburn wanted Higgins to do, no more, no less. That would have defused things

Cliff Thorburn is rightly famed for his granite-like strength of character. Yet even he – on occasion – can lose a match through loss of concentration

instantly. The incident would have struck everyone as a bit comical – a jest at the referee's expense. A bit of light relief in a tense match.

Instead, Higgins just looked dumbfounded. He appeared not to grasp the situation. His look of wide-eyed bewilderment was as transparent as Thorburn's mounting distress. What on earth was going on? The referee had called a foul. It was nothing to do with him. Why was Thorburn getting so steamed up? And getting steamed up he most certainly was. In the sense that it ever happens, steam was coming out of his ears.

Thorburn nearly exploded, not in that childish, whining, self-pitying way that some tennis players do with monotonous regularity, but as perfectly mature, strong-minded people do when they know they are victims of a monstrous miscarriage of justice. Such was Thorburn's visible rage that it is remarkable how well he managed to restrain himself. He was completely beside himself, yet he did not scream the house down and he did not throttle Higgins, which Higgins and a few million viewers must have thought on the cards as they witnessed such awesome fury.

The fatal effects of anger
What he did do was tamely surrender the match. It was way beyond even Thorburn's formidable powers of concentration to put the incident out of his mind and get on with the matter in hand. There could have been no better revenge than to punish his opponent at the table. However, by becoming maddened he had ruined his chances. No one's emotional

Matchplay temperament

resources are inexhaustible, and Thorburn had drawn on his too heavily. His concentration was out of the window, and his game could only follow. There are two morals to this story. First, nominate your ball loudly enough to be heard by the referee. The second moral is rather more serious: If you lose control, you lose.

It does not follow from this that you should go out of your way to achieve an ice-cool demeanor. There is nothing wrong with displaying a bit of emotion, although in matchplay you should be careful not to do so in a way that would disturb your opponent. Anger with yourself, when you have made a mess of things, is not only normal, it can be positively beneficial. You will never get anywhere if you are tolerant of your mistakes. On the contrary, you should be your own sternest critic. You know when you have done something stupid, and you should not let yourself get away with it. Give yourself a strict lecture. If that involves cursing yourself under your breath, go right ahead and curse yourself – under your breath. On the other hand, do not expect too much of yourself. At least make your opponent beat you rather than beat yourself through frustration.

Depending upon your natural temperament, you will be more or less inclined to display openly your annoyance with yourself. Some players find it a distraction to do so, preferring at all times to keep themselves on a tight rein. No matter how badly he has botched a shot (and he does, occasionally), Steve Davis never allows himself more than a

slight, rueful shake of the head, and not very often that. He prefers to mask his emotions behind that familiar impassive facade. That is the image he chooses to present to the world, and he cares nothing for the fact that many observers would warm more to him if he appeared a little looser, a little 'more human'. He probably considers that his demeanor gives him some psychological advantage against some of his opponents, but that, of course, is their problem. They are all after his scalp and he is perfectly entitled to use any fair

Steve Davis rarely betrays so much as a trace of his inner feelings. This imperturbable facade makes him an imposing figure – even when he is not at the table

means to protect that scalp.

Other players find it helps, more than it hurts, to keep the bottle not so tightly corked. It is very easy to tighten up physically during play, under pressure, and they know that to do so is fatal. For them, it is essential to let off a little steam now and then. Their display of annoyance

Fred Davis, grand old man of snooker, has always been a fierce competitor – despite that genial manner

with themselves acts as a safety-valve. That great champion of the 1950s and 60s, John Pulman, falls into this category, and he relates an amusing incident about it.

He was involved in an important match with Fred Davis, and he was playing badly. Nothing would go right. Davis would let him in with a chance, but after two or three pots he would break down. Pulman was getting really incensed about his bad form, angry that he was letting the match slip away through sheer incompetence. After one particular blunder, he could contain himself no longer. He stormed off through the doors and into the manager's office, where he proceeded to blow his top, against himself, of course.

There was a system whereby a buzzer in the manager's office would recall a player when his opponent broke down, and Pulman was just nicely settled into his tirade when the buzzer sounded. He was amazed by this, because he had left Davis in such a good position that a really big break seemed inevitable. But Davis had obviously broken down early on. Pulman swept back to the fray, but as he bounded into the hall he was greeted with a hail of laughter. When he looked at the table, Pulman could see nothing to laugh about. He was comprehensively snookered – snookered in behind the brown in such a way that even if he managed to escape and hit a red, he was virtually certain to let Davis in for a winning break. He did just that, and Davis serenely polished off the frame.

Why that burst of laughter, Pulman demanded to know, as he and Davis went off for the interval? The genial Davis explained. Having messed up his position on the break, he had just trickled up to the brown for that deadly snooker. As he returned to his seat, just a split second before Pulman hurtled through the doors, he had remarked to the crowd: 'Fasten your safety-belts.'

Regardless of how you manage to deal with tension and pressure, you must never allow yourself to lose concentration. You must concentrate from beginning to end, no mean feat in a long match, but you must discipline yourself to do it. At the higher levels of play, a single lapse in concentration can prove fatal. In a friendly game with an equal, it can turn the scales. You must concentrate when you are not at the table as much as when you are. Always watch your opponent at play. There are two reasons for this. First, you may discover his weaknesses, and then go on to exploit them when it is your turn to play. Second, it helps to keep distracting thoughts at bay.

Play positive snooker

You must adopt and retain a positive attitude to playing snooker. Snooker is a game of attack and defence, subtly blended depending upon the circumstances as they evolve during the course of play. However, it is always a positive game, whether the circumstances at any particular stage favour an offensive or defensive stroke. A killing safety shot is every bit as positive as a winning pot.

It is impossible in the pages of a book to give specific advice for the specific situations that you will encounter in the course of your snooker-playing career, but you may find a few general comments helpful. Safety play is a vital aspect of the game, but do not make a fetish of it. Insomuch as snooker can be reduced to a single, bedrock element, it is about potting balls. Do not get into the habit of declining reasonable potting opportunities just because you might miss them. Players who do that will never make much progress. This is not to say that you should throw caution to the winds as you step to the table. You should not make unreasonable demands on your potting skill, and you should not despise good opportunities to make life difficult for your opponent. But, most of the time, at any level of snooker, the best way to discomfort your opponent is to run away from him on the scoreboard. Knock in a good break early on in a frame and you are in business.

Players who adopt an aggressive approach (to the balls on the table) always win admirers. John Parrott, a rising star, is firmly in this mould

You will feel confident and your opponent will feel pressure. Knock in another later on and you will probably win the frame. Keep applying that sort of pressure and you both demoralize and intimidate your opponent. That is really what snooker is all about.

You might think from your experience of watching televised snooker that not all the players adopt such an approach. You would be wrong. They all do, from 'Whirlwind' White to 'Steady Eddie' Charlton. Of course White looks thrilling in attack, and Charlton sometimes dour in defence. White is the better potter. Most experts would say, indeed do say, that he is the most naturally gifted potter the game has ever seen. That being so, it means that he realistically sees reasonable potting opportunities where others, just as realistically, do not. Simply trying to out-pot White would be to fall into the trap of playing him at his own game – the game at which he is best, although he has had some marvellous shoot-outs with another gifted young potter, Kirk Stevens. His opponents beat him, when they do, by playing their own game, at their own pace. They play within themselves, as they should. But they all play aggressively, as they must do to stand any chance of winning at that level. At your level, the same truth holds.

Not only will excessive devotion to safety play inhibit your progress as a player, it will stifle your enjoyment. Snooker is, after all, only a game, and games are supposed to be fun. Bold players are bound to have more fun than timid ones. It is a lovely feel-ing to make a difficult pot, and how can you experience that feeling if you always duck the challenge? How wretched the game would become if you scuttled for safety the whole time, priding yourself on the fact that while you may not be scoring, your opponent is making no headway either.

The professionals see it the same way, even with so much at stake. A cautious attitude is not what stirred them to take up the game in the first place, develop such a passion for it and set out to conquer the world. Griffiths could be speaking for all of them when he says that he can bear to play an attacking game and lose, even if the loss is directly caused by a risky attacking shot that fails to come off. But he absolutely detests losing if he has been put on the defensive and has allowed himself to remain there without striking out boldly for victory. Whenever you find negative thoughts creeping into your mind, as of course they will, try to remember the old adage: 'Fortune favours the brave.' Or the new one: 'Go for it!' Win or lose, that is the way to play.

'Steady Eddie' Charlton is formidable in defence, but that does not account for his great playing record. Like all the top players, he must attack to win

Chapter 7 SNOOKER RULES

The phenomenal popularity of televised snooker has made the basic rules very widely known, even by many who have never played the game. The complete novice is therefore quite likely to know the basic rules outlined below – the rules that enable you to know what is going on in a game, and to approach the table knowing at least the sort of thing you should be attempting to do. There are, however, common situations which crop up in the course of a game that can only be resolved by reference to quite complicated rules – rules that are frequently not known or misinterpreted by many players, even good players. Examples of these, but examples only, follow the basic rules.

The basic rules

Snooker is played with twenty two balls, fifteen reds, six different colours and a white cue ball. At the start of a game (a frame), the reds are positioned in a triangle above and as close as possible to, but without touching, the pink which is sitting on its spot. The other coloured balls are on their respective spots as well, while the cue ball is placed anywhere within the 'D' for the first stroke. Thereafter, the cue ball must be played from where it rests on the table except when it has been accidentally potted (gone in-off) or been forced off the table. In those cases the following player must play from within the 'D'.

Points are scored in two ways. The principal means is by potting balls. On each trip to the table a player must first attempt to strike a red (as long as there remain reds on the table). If he pots it he scores one point, and he must then attempt to strike any one of the colours. He must nominate the colour he is attempting to hit, although this rule is ignored where the choice is obvious. If there could be the slightest doubt, he must nominate. Potting the various coloured balls score: yellow (2), green (3), brown (4), blue (5), pink (6), black (7). Whereas potted reds stay down

in the pockets, a potted colour is replaced on its spot, and the player must play on another red. If he succeeds in potting another red, he is back on the colours, any colour (including the one he just potted), and so on until he fails to pot a ball. Then it is the next player's turn. The game proceeds in this manner until all the reds have been potted. Then the colours must be potted in ascending order of value, from yellow to black. The final disappearance of the black, leaving only the cue ball on the table, marks the end of the game save when the scores are level. In this instance the black is re-spotted and the players toss a coin for choice of first shot with the cue ball placed anywhere in the 'D'.

Foul strokes

The other means of accumulating points is through your opponent's foul strokes. Failure to strike a red incurs a penalty of four points, unless the cue ball strikes a ball of higher value than that (blue, pink or black), in which case the penalty is the value of that ball. Failure to strike the nominated colour also brings a penalty of four points, except where the colour is of higher value, in which case again the penalty is that value.

If in failing to hit a low-value colour the cue ball hits a high-value colour, he is penalized at the higher value. Going in-off costs four points, more if it results from a shot on one of the high-value colours. After an in-off, the next player plays from within the 'D'.

All these fouls, and consequent penalties, can be attributed to mistakes, or carelessness, but an important aspect of the game is the deliberate laying of snookers – leaving your opponent in such a position that he has no direct line of play to a ball he must hit. He is then forced either to swerve the cue ball or play it off one or more cushions en route to the object ball. Depending upon the difficulty of the snooker he may well miss, may probably miss or may almost certainly miss. As well as giving you between four and seven penalty points, this can be of great tactical significance.

Should a player find himself snookered on the reds following a foul shot by his opponent, he may nominate any colour as a red. This is called a 'free ball'. If he pots it he scores one, as though it were a red, and then he chooses a colour in the normal way. If there are no reds remaining, the free ball has the value

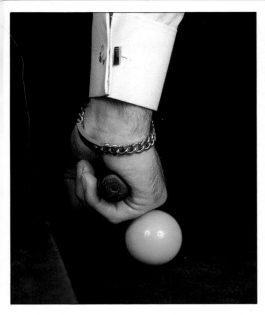

of the lowest value colour on the table, and if he pots it he must proceed with the colours in sequence, in the normal way.

In addition to those described so far, the following are all fouls:

1 Playing with both feet off the floor.
2 Playing before all the balls have come to rest.
3 Double striking on the cue ball.
4 Touching the cue ball with anything other than the cue tip (an article of clothing, for instance — simply touching, even if the cue ball is not disturbed).
5 Playing with the balls wrongly spotted.
6 Jumping the cue ball over any other ball.
7 Knocking any ball off the table.

The complete set of rules for snooker should be prominently posted in every snooker hall and club, but sadly that is not the case. Even where they are posted, the darkened atmosphere of the room does not encourage the reading of fine print. The fine print is important, and it would be sensible of you to buy a copy from your nearest supplier of equipment — if, that is, he stocks it. Failing that, you can write direct to: The Billiards and Snooker Control Council, Coronet House, Queen St, Leeds LS1 2TN.

Touching a ball accidentally (top left) is a foul, and Ray Reardon had better exercise his customary caution. That yellow ball is perilously close to his waistcoat

The pink flies through the air and off the table — a six-point foul, of a type that causes merriment amongst the spectators even in a tense match

Complicated rules

Most of the confusions about the rules of snooker occur because the rules were laid down on the assumption that the game would invariably be refereed. The referee envisaged was not just a friend of the two players, acting like a scorer in a game of darts, but a properly qualified certificated referee. He would understand thoroughly every particular of the rules, and his application of them would be accepted in a sporting spirit (as witness the professional game). Under such circumstances, individual players could take as much or as little interest in the more complicated rules as they wished. They would merely have to comply.

The realities of snooker-playing contrast starkly with this. The vast majority of games are unrefereed, necessarily so, and always will be. In some cases this makes it impossible, practically speaking, to enforce the rules. For example, you might touch the cue ball with an article of clothing and be quite unaware of the fact, and therefore unable to call the foul against yourself (which you would in fairness be obliged to do if

Might Tony Knowles accidentally touch the cue ball as he addresses it (below)? Does the pink re-spot cleanly (below right), and is the cue ball correctly repositioned after being cleaned (bottom)? The referee's keen eye is essential

you did notice it). You would consider your opponent to have an unsporting attitude if he watched you like a hawk every time you addressed the ball, on the off chance of spotting such a misdemeanour. And if he did so, you might dispute it hotly. Then who would judge?

For the rest, the fact that you will be playing without a referee, except possibly on occasion, means that you really must get to grips with the rules. And you must hope to play against opponents who understand them too, because controversies stemming from ignorance will spoil the enjoyment of a game. There follow some typical examples of the practical application of the rules of snooker.

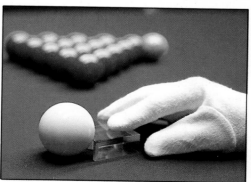

Re-spotting the balls

As long as there remain reds on the table, it is a foul to play a stroke with a colour missing. It does not matter whether it was you, or your opponent, or even a referee who failed to re-spot the missing colour. Nor does it matter when the oversight occurred. The moment it comes to light, whoever notices it, the player who has just played is adjudged to have fouled, and to have fouled at that moment. In other words, should it be discovered in the course of a break, all strokes prior to that, and therefore the score accumulated to that last stroke, are considered good. It is also a foul stroke to play when a colour has been re-spotted on the wrong spot. Again, the penalty is applied against the player in play when the mistake is discovered, even if it was not he who incorrectly re-spotted the ball.

When the spots are covered

In the course of a game it is common for one of the spots to become covered, or partially covered, by another ball. If a colour cannot be re-spotted cleanly (without touching another ball) on its own spot, it is re-spotted on the highest value spot unoccupied (black, pink and so on down the order to yellow). If all the spots are occupied, it is placed as near its own spot as possible, without touching another ball, and in a direct line with the nearest point of the top cushion. Take the blue, for example. It would be placed as near as possible to its spot without touching another ball, between that and the pink spot and in a direct line with the pink and black spots.

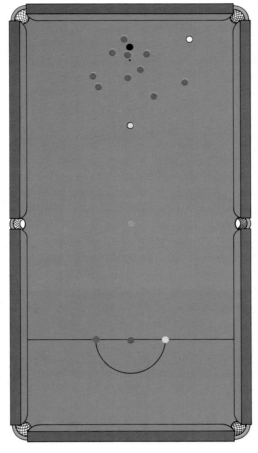

All the spots are covered, so the black is re-spotted as near its own spot as possible, without touching another ball, in direct line with the nearest point on the top cushion

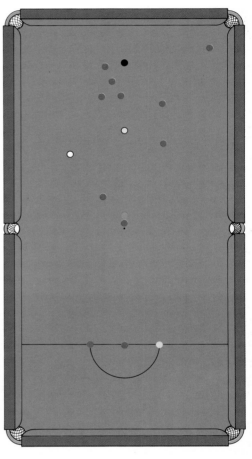

With all the spots covered, the blue is re-spotted as near its own spot as possible, directly in line with the pink and black spots

A snooker

Most players think they understand well enough what a snooker is, and for the most part that knowledge is sufficient, although it is likely to be incomplete. It is generally reckoned that you are snookered if you cannot hit both sides of the ball 'on'. Strictly speaking, this is not the case. If it were, you would be snookered when breaking off, because you cannot hit both sides of any red in the triangle. You are in fact snookered when a ball not 'on' prevents you from hitting both sides of the ball 'on'. You cannot, of course, be snookered by another ball 'on'. That is, you cannot be snookered on a red by a red.

You are snookered even if you can hit enough of the ball 'on' to pot it. Under those circumstances, the fact that you are technically snookered may not concern you, but it becomes important if such a situation arises after a foul stroke by your opponent. You may take on the pot, or you may opt for a free ball. If you take on the

Steve Davis finds himself comprehensively snookered on the reds, and is contemplating the means of escape

pot, you have waived your right to a free ball. You cannot, say, hit the intervening ball and claim it retroactively as a free ball. If you nominate a free ball you must not only hit it before hitting any other ball, you must not lay a snooker behind it. If you do, you have fouled. This is an important rule because it prevents you from trickling the cue ball up behind a free ball to snooker your opponent. You are, of course, entitled to play off the free ball so as to snooker your opponent behind another ball. And you are entitled to use the free ball to help you pot a ball that is 'on', for instance as a plant, as long as you hit the free ball first.

The touching ball

Nothing in snooker causes as much confusion as the touching ball rule. One aspect of it appears at first glance to be contradictory, and so it will always seem until you fix it firmly in your mind. First, the uncontradictory aspect of the rule. The cue ball must be played away from the ball it is touching without disturbing it. Otherwise it is a foul.

Now to the confusing bit. If the cue ball is touching a ball that is 'on', whether red or colour, then in the act of playing away from it a player is deemed to have played it. He may send the cue ball where he likes, without touching another ball, and he has played a lawful stroke. If, on the other hand, the cue ball is touching a ball that is not 'on' (either red or colour), then in the act of playing away from it he is deemed not to have played it, because otherwise it would be a foul stroke. He is obliged to hit a ball that is 'on', or it is a foul stroke.

Suppose you are touching a red and 'on' a red. You can play away from the touching red to pot another red, or to lay a snooker elsewhere on the table, with or without hitting any other ball (always assuming that you do not disturb the touching red). If there are no reds left and you are touching the yellow and 'on' the yellow you must attempt a safety shot, preferably a snooker, because there is no ball for you to pot. You would automatically foul by disturbing the yellow – unless you initially played away and struck it via a cushion. In a situation where the reds are gone, the colours all remaining and you are touching the black, you must hit the yellow, even if you are snookered on it.

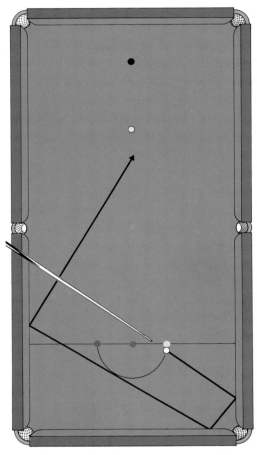

With the cue ball touching the yellow and 'on' yellow, the only option is to play away from it in an attempt to reach safety

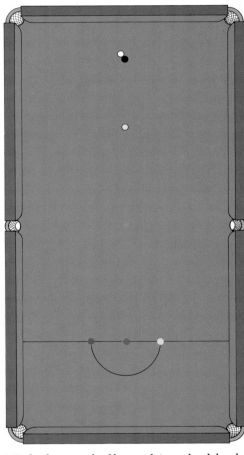

With the cue ball touching the black and 'on' yellow, the player must hit the yellow – in this case by negotiating a fiendish snooker

The last two colours

It is obviously the intention of the rules to ensure that a player can never gain an advantage over his opponent by fouling. If he could, it would lead to deliberate fouling, which would change the nature of the game in an unthinkable direction. There is one particular instance in which the free ball rule, as explained so far, could give rise to just that. Only pink and black remain on the table, your opponent has just fouled, but even with the penalty forfeit you are still more than thirteen points behind and therefore require a snooker to win. In the course of fouling, he has snookered you on the pink, thereby giving you a free ball. What are you to do? You must nominate the black, and if the black happens to be in a good potting position all is well, because it would be re-spotted after you pot it. If not, you are in deep trouble because the free ball rule

prevents you from laying a snooker behind the black. You must simply play it safe. Worse, suppose the pink is in an easy potting position. Your opponent has you at his mercy, and all because of the outcome of that foul stroke. To remedy that defect in the free ball rule, it has been altered to exempt this unique situation from it. When only pink and black remain, it is permissible for a player to lay a snooker behind the black.

This is the exception to the rule that you cannot lay a snooker behind a nominated free ball. With only pink and black remaining, you are entitled to lay a snooker behind the black

Miscellaneous points

1 There is a popular misconception that the game is not properly under-way until the cue ball disturbs the pack of reds. Should the player making the first stroke miss the pack entirely, he thinks that he must play the shot again from the 'D'. This is entirely wrong. The game begins the moment the cue tip strikes the cue ball on the opening shot. Missing the reds is a foul with the appropriate penalty (four, unless the cue ball hits one of the higher colours). It is now the next player's turn to play on the reds – and if he is snookered the free ball rule is applied, even at this stage.

2 If a ball is forced on to a cushion rail, runs along it and then drops back on to the table, all is well. If it is an 'on' ball and it runs right along the cushion rail to drop into the pocket, it counts as a good pot. If it remains on the cushion rail it is a foul, just as though it had been forced right off the table. The penalty is either its own value or the value of the ball 'on', whichever is the higher. If it is a red, it is put in a pocket, as it would be if it were knocked off the table. If it is a colour it is re-spotted. If it is the cue ball it is played from the 'D' (by the next player).

3 Occasionally, a ball may hover tantalizingly on the edge of a pocket before falling in. If it does so only momentarily, it is counted as in (whether a pot or an in-off). If, how-ever, it falls in later, without being touched, it is replaced on the edge of the pocket. If it falls in during the course of a shot, the balls involved are all replaced and the shot is taken again, without penalty.

The 'Professional Rule'

There can be many instances in a game in which a player could gain an advantage through fouling, despite giving away the requisite number of points. There is a rule prohibiting an intentional miss on a ball 'on', but this not only requires a referee to adjudge, it also poses a terrible dilemma. Was it a deliberate miss or just a rotten shot? Was he cheating (for to call it a deliberate miss would be to say no less than that), or was he simply lucky to gain an advantage from an incompetent shot? This is not the only type of foul that could result in injury to the innocent party. Suppose with only pink and black left, a player goes in-off and, by some weird but by no means impossible fluke, leaves the black hanging over the pocket with the pink so close to it that by moving the pink his opponent is bound to pot the black. That fluke result of a foul would decide the game in favour of its perpetrator.

'Play again, please'

Many years ago, the professionals decided to take this element of luck and potential controversy out of their game by adding an additional rule – the so-called 'Professional Rule' as it was then known. You see it applied all the time on television and it has long since been added to the official rules. It is a rule of beautiful simplicity. It states that following a foul stroke, the next player has the right to make his opponent play again. It does not matter what type of foul stroke it was, or what stage the game is at. It has no effect whatever on the free ball rule. But just as a foul can leave you unsnookered but in a nasty

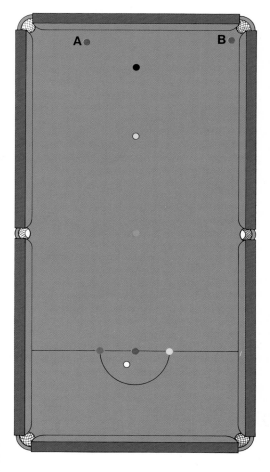

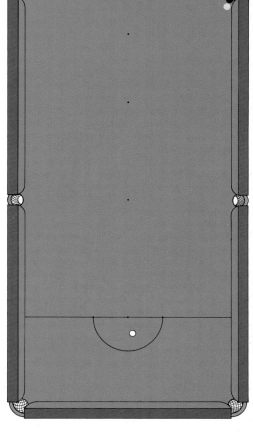

position, so it can leave you with a free ball that is of no use to you. It can leave you with a shot you would find difficult to play in such a way as to achieve safety. In such a case, you apply the 'Professional Rule' and ask your opponent to take the shot. Remember that the rule can be applied at any stage of the game – including the break-off, where it is entirely possible for a player to go in-off and leave his opponent unhappily positioned on the reds from anywhere in the 'D'.

Examples of the 'Professional Rule' following a foul. Above left, if Red B is on the table, this is a case for asking your opponent to play again. It would be miraculous if he (or you) could play Red A and emerge safe on Red B. If Red B were not there, however, you might send Red A to safety (even achieving a snooker) off top and left side cushions. Above, your opponent has gone in-off, leaving you with the virtually impossible task of hitting the pink without knocking in the black. Enforce the rule

Glossary

Backspin
The effect of striking the cue ball below centre.

Break
A sequence of scoring shots.

Break-off
The opening shot of a frame in which the striker must play at the triangle of reds.

Check side
Side-spin that narrows the angle at which the cue ball rebounds from the cushion.

Clearance
A sequence of scoring shots which continues until the player has potted all the balls left on the table.

'D'
The semicircle inscribed on the baulk line from which all strokes must be played when the striker is in hand (eg. when breaking off).

Double
A shot by which the object ball is potted after striking one or more cushions.

Double-kiss
A second contact on the object ball.

Drag shot
A long shot that is played with normal strength and plenty of backspin, the effect being to slow down the cue ball late in its journey.

Fluke
A shot that results in a fortuitous bonus (for example, an unintentional pot or snooker).

Forcing shot
A stroke played considerably above medium pace.

Foul stroke
A shot or action that infringes one of the rules of snooker, thereby incurring a specified penalty.

Free ball
The result of a snooker caused by a foul stroke. The player snookered in this way (ie, he cannot hit both extremities of the object ball) may nominate any coloured ball as a red for the purposes of his next shot. If he pots it he scores one, and then nominates a colour in the usual manner. If there are no reds left on the table, he nominates one of the colours as a free ball, and if he pots it he scores the value of the lowest value ball on the table. The nominated colour is re-spotted and he then plays the colours in sequence.

Full-ball contact
Striking the object ball full face, so that all of it is covered by the cue ball at the moment of impact.

Half-ball contact
Striking the object ball so that half of it is covered by the cue ball at the moment of impact.

Half butt
A matching 7½ft cue and rest required to reach the cue ball for any shots too distant to reach with the normal rest.

In-off
A shot resulting in the cue ball being pocketed (and therefore a foul stroke).

Kick
An unclear contact between cue ball and object ball, caused by chalk, dust or anything that results in the de-glossing of a portion of one of the balls. It distorts the angle of deflection, and sometimes causes the cue ball to lift off slightly.

Kiss
Contact by the cue ball on a second (or subsequent) object ball.

Massé
A shot in which the cue strikes almost vertically down on one side of the cue ball, imparting maximum swerve. It is much more common in billiards than snooker.

Maximum break
A scoring sequence in which the player pots all fifteen reds, fifteen blacks and all the colours to score a maximum total of 147.

Natural angle
The angle the cue ball will take after striking the object ball at medium pace without spin of any sort.

Plain ball
Centre striking of the cue ball (ie, no topspin, backspin or side).

Plant
A position in which one object ball is played on to another object ball in order to pot the latter.

Pocket weight
A slow shot carrying pace just sufficient to carry the object ball to the pocket.

Power shot
A forcing shot of great pace.

Quarter-ball contact
Striking the object ball so that one quarter of it is covered by the cue ball at the moment of impact.

Rest
The smallest and least cumbersome of the implements used to reach the cue ball when it is beyond comfortable range for a conventional bridge.

Running side
Side-spin that widens the angle at which the cue ball rebounds from the cushion.

Safe position
A lie from which a scoring stroke is unlikely.

Safety shot
A defensive stroke that aims not to score but to leave the opponent in a safe position.

Screw
To impart backspin to the cue ball, the result being a stun, screw or drag shot, depending upon factors of distance and pace.

Screw shot
A shot in which the cue ball recoils from the object ball upon contact (if full ball), or leaves it at wider than the natural angle if angled contact.

Set
A type of plant in which the two object balls are touching.

Shot to nothing
A tactical shot whereby the player attempts to pot the ball in such a way as to leave himself in a position to continue the break should he succeed with the pot, but leaving his opponent in a safe position should he fail.

Side-spin
Called simply side, it is the effect of striking the cue ball off centre (right or left). It will either widen or narrow the angle at which the cue ball rebounds from a cushion, and can be used in conjunction with either backspin or topspin.

Snooker
A lie from which the player is unable to hit both sides of the object ball by an intervening ball that is not 'on'.

Spider
A rest with a raised head, allowing bridging at a distance over an intervening ball or balls. There are variations, devised for particularly awkward positions.

Stun shot
A shot in which the cue ball stops dead upon contact with the object ball (if full ball), or leaves it at a wider than normal angle (but not as wide as a screw shot) if angled contact. Stun shots usually require the application of screw, but where the cue ball and object ball are very close together stun may be achieved by central striking or even slightly higher.

Stun run-through shot
A shot at close quarters where the object is to retard the cue ball's forward momentum after contact with the object ball, but not kill it totally.

Swerve
Exaggerated side-spin, achieved by striking down on one side of the cue ball, the object being to curve the cue ball around an obstructing ball.

Three-quarter-ball contact
Striking the object ball so that three-quarters of it is covered by the cue ball at the moment of impact.

Three-quarter butt
A 9ft version of the half butt, mercifully needed only rarely.

Topspin
The effect achieved by striking the cue ball above centre.

Index

Numerals in *italics* refer to illustrations

Acknowledgements

We would like to thank A & D Billiards & Pool Services Ltd for providing the picture on page 8 and David Muscroft Picture Library for supplying the cover pictures and all other photographs used in the book.

Our thanks also to Silvino Francisco for appearing in several of the instructional photographs.